lost and found
IN THE LAND OF
MAÑANA

WILDHEARTED LIVING IN AN IMPERFECT WORLD

CHRISSY GRUNINGER

A *for Harmony* Publication © 2017

All Rights Reserved.

This book is also available on iTunes and Kindle.

This book, or parts thereof, may not be reproduced in any form without permission of the author.

Photograph of author by Cara Koch / La Vida in Life Photography

Praise for Lost and Found in the Land of Mañana

Lost and Found in the Land of Mañana reveals the ups and downs of what it really takes be fully alive. Chrissy's stories about moving to Costa Rica and finding herself in a very different world from what she had always known shows us that with a little effort, courage and an open mind, we can choose happiness, even amongst all the difficulties we face in the day to day. While her story is about living in Costa Rica, what she shares, the lessons she learns, can be applied to anyone, anywhere. Chrissy reminds us that adversity, failure and mishaps are all just stepping stones to a purposeful, beautiful life.

Colin Beavan, AKA No Impact Man
Author, How to Be Alive

Chrissy reflects the reality for all of us: that life is what we make of it. Her stories of feeling lost and confused remind us that even if we're "living the dream life", not everything will go as planned and result in the perfect happily-ever-after ending.

Lost and Found in the Land of Mañana is a genuine, vulnerable book that will have you laughing, crying and even contemplating how you can do more, in your own life and out in the world. Without a doubt, Chrissy is a SavvyChick, who not only has learned how to live a good life on her own terms but wants to share those lessons with others.

Rosalie Nelson
Founder, SavvyChick.com

Lost and Found in the Land of Mañana is an eye-opening book on what it's really like to live abroad. While we may dream of what living in paradise is like...the superficial, sitting on the beach, drinking a cocktail and soaking up the sunshine...is really just a fantasy. The substance of actually living a wholehearted life in the everyday chaos is what, through her stories and actions, Chrissy shows us how to do. No matter where we are, we all face challenges and it's how we show up and turn them into meaningful moments that make all the difference.

Charlotte Watts
Author, The De-Stress Effect

WINNER: BEST MEMOIR

Also by Chrissy Gruninger

Rich Coast Experiences Collection

Vicarious Adventures on the Rich Coast

No Fear

Lost and Found in the Land of Mañana

Living Well Collection

A Wildhearted Sanguine Life

An Intentional Life

An Interconnected Life

A Harmonious Life

Nourishing Wisdom

Living Intentionally

Daily Yoga

Lost and Found in the Land of Mañana
Wildhearted living in an imperfect world

Intro: How a California Girl Came to Call Costa Rica Home

- Ch. 1: Outside My Comfort Zone
- Ch. 2: Cooking, Cleaning, Shopping
- Ch. 3: The Creepy Crawlies
- Ch. 4: The New Normal
- Ch. 5: Every Rose Has Its Thorn
- Ch. 6: Pura Vida?
- Ch. 7: Oh, Nachiruro
- Ch. 8: Business As (Un)usual
- Ch. 9: Real Life on the Rich Coast
- Ch. 10: Swimming Upstream

PART 1: LOST
PART 2: FOUND

- Ch. 11: Finding Myself
- Ch. 12: Letting Go
- Ch. 13: Acceptance
- Ch. 14: Self Growth
- Ch. 15: Self Care
- Ch. 16: Gratitude
- Ch. 17: Lovingkindness
- Ch. 18: Moderation
- Ch. 19: Abundance
- Ch. 20: Authenticity
- Ch. 21: Wildhearted Harmony

Epilogue: The Present Moment

Introduction 1

PART 1: LOST 9

Ch 1: The First Hundred Days of My New Life..... 11
Ch 2: Learning to Grocery Shop and Cook
       All Over Again.. 26
Ch 3: Making Friends With The Creepy Crawlies 47
Ch 4: But It's Not Just About The Bugs & The Food:
       The New Normal 60
Ch 5: Every Rose Has Its Thorn........................... 79
Ch 6: Does "Pura Vida" Mean What
       You Think It Means?................................. 101
Ch 7: Oh Machismo... You're Just Not Needed.. 112
Ch 8: I'm Sure You've Guessed It By Now,
       Doing Business Here Sucks 135
Ch 9: Real on the Rich Coast: the Good...
       and the Not So Ideal 147
Ch 10: Swimming Upstream in The Land
        of Mañana... 156

Part 2 – Found 165

Ch 11: Introduction.. 167
Ch 12: Surrender 179
Ch 13: Acceptance 191
Ch 14: Self-Growth 203
Ch 15: Self-Care... 222
Ch 16: Gratitude.. 235
Ch 17: Lovingkindness....................................... 240
Ch 18: Moderation 248

Ch 19: Abundance 259
Ch 20: Authenticity 265
Ch 21: Wildhearted Harmony 277

Epilogue: the present moment 297

Gratitude

Just like life, this book has had a lot of twists and turns (and even a few upside down backflips). It was most definitely not the easiest one to write.

It is with so much gratitude that it is finally out in the world, sharing my story, with the hope of lifting up and inspiring others to live their ONE beautiful life, on their own terms.

There are many wonderful people in my life who I am grateful for but in this note of *Gratitude*, I wanted to focus on just a few who, in their own way, have helped me bring this book to life.

First off, my awesome editor Kieta who stepped up at the eleventh hour to make sure this book got into the world.

My dear friend Miriam, while you live so very far away, I always feel your presence and support by my side.

Julia B, because you were a guest leader in a retreat in 2007, I met Troy. And from there, more ripples were created that eventually led me to living here. Had that retreat not happened, well, who knows how my life story would have unfolded.

Mike, you will always be my BFF. Thank you for storing all my precious items that I just couldn't let go of. Only a few more years and those not-so-precious tax returns can be shredded.

Dr. Koval, way back when, you taught me so many of the concepts I apply now on how to live my one beautiful life, show up every day and mentor others to do the same. I am grateful for the lessons you taught and the guidance and support you gave to me.

As you may notice in this book, I also have deep reverence for the yoga sutras of Patanjali. These are life philosophies I have been studying since 2002 when I realized there was so much more to yoga than what we do "on the mat". Still, more than a decade later, I recognize there is always more to learn...

Dedication

For those who choose to do more than just live in "*Margaritaville*".

Who want to show up and live their ONE beautiful life with meaning.

Fully and freely.

Wildheartedly.

"What is joy without sorrow?
What is success without failure?
What is a win without a loss?
What is health without illness?
You have to experience each
if you are to appreciate the other.
There is always
going to be suffering.
It's how you look at your suffering,
how you deal with it,
that will define you."

Mark Twain

INTRODUCTION

"Throw your dreams into space like a kite, and you do not know what it will bring back, a new life, a new friend, a new love, a new country."

Anais Nin

LOST AND FOUND IN THE LAND OF MAÑANA

Bienvenidos al tercer libro de mis aventuras y lecciones en la hermosa Costa Rica.

I've been in Costa Rica for a few years now, and though I spoke a passable amount of Spanish when I first arrived, I believe I've now earned the right to at least *start* my book *en* ESPAÑOL. It's a privilege and honor to be crafting a third book about my adventures and lessons, and to have the opportunity to bring some closure to some of the issues that got me writing about Costa Rica in the first place.

If you've been following along with my last two books, you know I have an intense love for the Rich Coast since my first trip in 2006. It's where I feel the most healthy, which in turn gives me an overall sense of peace and well-being, of being whole and comfortable in my surroundings, a sense of being at *home*.

I wasn't healthy in California. I'd seen all kinds of doctors, conventional and holistic, and no one could pinpoint exactly what the issues were, but they could all see the intense misery and pain I was in on a daily, never-ending basis. My only reprieve was visiting tropical, warm, humid countries. I would count the days until my next holiday in Costa Rica, Nicaragua, Panama, or even dilapidated but beautiful Cuba - anywhere that was warm and humid.

I wondered:

"What would it feel like to wake up each day in a warm, tropical environment and actually feel healthy? To live at the beach and enjoy summer year-round? And beyond that day to day reality... What would it be like to soar into the unknown and do it all on my own?"

I was finally granted a reprieve after my tenth visit when I was hired by a hospitality management firm. I knew I had finally found a way to move to Costa Rica permanently. Somehow, fear never entered my mind with this decision to take a leap of faith. I knew deep in my soul that Costa Rica was where I wanted to be.

I spent the following year planning for the next chapter in my life to begin, and I thought I had everything planned out (but trust me, I didn't) In the cold never-ending winter of 2012, I was dreaming of what my life would be like when I could finally say, "*Vivo en Costa Rica.*"

While I gave up many modern-day conveniences with the move, I regained my health. My energy level went from feeling like an 80-year-old, confined to my house, to that of a 22-year-old with a newfound vibrancy for life. Trust me when I say, if you don't have your health, you don't have a life. I know that I'm so very blessed to live the life I have now.

Sundresses and Sandals was the working title I came up with for this book long before I actually had the experiences to fill it. I dreamed of the adventures I'd have, blissfully flaunting my newly improved health and beautiful new life on the Rich Coast. When I think about that time, so bright eyed and naïve, I smirk a little. And laugh. I've found laughing at myself to be an indispensable tool for coping with life in a completely different culture.

My friends in Costa Rica warned me that life here would be nothing like I expected and absolutely nothing like vacationing here. I believed them with a somewhat doe-eyed innocence. In truth, I hoped to be the exception; I hoped that sitting in the bank for hours on end wouldn't bother me or better yet, wouldn't happen. I was pretty sure that they were all exaggerating when they shared their stories of the never-ending frustrations of living in what the majority of the world thinks of as paradise. After all, Costa Rica and I had an understanding. We'd been flirting hard-core for years and we'd finally made it Facebook official. They'd all see.

These last few years, I've learned a lot. About myself, about my never-ending resilience, about life, love and loss. A few months into living here, a friend told me: *"Chrissy, this country will beat you down."* And it did. Repeatedly. Again and again. And continues to do so. There is nothing simple about life on the Rich Coast. Not for foreigners. Not even really for *Ticos (the term Costa Rican's call themselves)*, it seems. We all seem to accept that it's a crazy place and for one reason or another, we all choose to stay.

These are my stories of fear, love, intense adventures, and solid plans gone wildly awry.

They encapsulate my infinite desire to know, understand, and appreciate all that life has to offer. To find my path, the middle way, the embodiment of mindfulness and non-attachment (both physically and mentally). To surrender to the unknown beauty of living every day while being present and aware, even when conditions around me prove challenging. They're evidence of my personal quest to continuously improve my ability to adapt, improvise, and overcome. To be empowered to live wildheartedly. Harmoniously.

While some of the stories may seem like I'm making generalizations about an entire country, I want to be clear that I have met many amazing people in Costa Rica. My experiences of running (sometimes headfirst) into cultural differences are not meant to paint a picture of Costa Ricans as crazy, backwards and upside down people - merely that my interactions often felt that way when our worldviews didn't line up.

Committing to my love for Costa Rica and confining our long distance affair to a residency hasn't been easy, but like any love worth having, I find the challenge helps us grow together rather than apart.

Each morning, I open my eyes to a day that I know will contain both the pleasant and the not so pleasant, the good and the bad, the joy and the sadness, the glory and the defeat — that's inevitable. That, is life.

Embracing the practice of what I like to call *a sanguine life* means accepting the good and the not-so-ideal that comes my way, and learning to trust that all of it is there for a reason.

If I am truly going to embrace my life, I have to embrace all that Costa Rica brings to the table. To truly lead a sanguine life, I let the good times increase my buoyancy of spirit, creating reserves that help carry me up and over challenges (and give others a boost along the way too). My cheerful optimism lights my path even as the dark clouds roll in.

During moments of peace and ease, I feel comfortable where I am, in my bare feet. My little patch of grass is the greenest I've ever seen.

However, it hasn't always been that way.

My story starts in California, where my life was good. Meaningful. A fly on the wall wouldn't have said otherwise. But I had a strong inkling that I had more to offer to the world (and myself!). So I made a change. A really big change. And part of me hoped that I'd ride off into the sunset, happily ever after. It was a disappointment when vitality and wellness did NOT immediately follow. The profound harmony I had anticipated gave way to darkness — yes, even in paradise — that cast a shadow over me for the first two years here.

My heart knew that Costa Rica was the right place for me, and despite my freedom from illness, I began to feel lost. I was off-kilter, not at one with myself or my surroundings. Where was my zen-in-paradise fantasy?

> I knew then that it was up to me. Costa Rica could only do so much and it was time to uphold my end of the bargain.

And so I began the slow, intentional process of healing myself — all of the parts that were hurting and lost — and learning to take all of life (the sunshine and the rain) together as pieces of a beautiful, messy puzzle. Good days happen and bad days happen, and when I am at my most sanguine, I am buoyed by my inner harmony, and lovingly supported by the earth beneath my feet. I've learned to love every step of this journey that brought me to this place and I'm so excited to now share those steps with you.

So now, grab a green drink or a glass of wine, sit back, and enjoy this bumpy ride on what I call the rocky, twisting road of my life here in the land of mañana...

LOST AND FOUND IN THE LAND OF MAÑANA

CHRISSY GRUNINGER

PART 1: LOST

LOST AND FOUND IN THE LAND OF MAÑANA

Chapter 1
The First Hundred Days of My New Life

"One's philosophy is not best expressed in words; it is expressed in the choices one makes... and the choices we make are ultimately our responsibility."

Eleanor Roosevelt

LOST AND FOUND IN THE LAND OF MAÑANA

It was an unseasonably warm day in March of 2008, and I was sitting on the Point Reyes Seashore with a couple of friends. Then and there I made the declaration: *"I will move to Costa Rica."* They both kind of stared at me, mouths open. Then they smiled. Then they laughed. They were most likely thinking, *"How is she ever going to do that? That's just crazy talk. Crazy Chrissy and her wild ideas."*

It wasn't that I was unhappy in California. After all, I lived in beautiful Sonoma County with vineyards, giant old-growth redwoods, and rugged coastal beaches. My mind and spirit were happy there, but my body never felt well. However, during the two times I had visited Costa Rica, I felt free, healthy, and a sense of total, wildhearted oneness - like everything was right in the world.

Admittedly, falling for a guy during my second trip may have had a little something to do with my newfound desire to move. I won't pretend that I didn't envision myself with him on sandy beaches, going for hikes, and enjoying picnics together shaded by almendra trees.

But let the record clearly state that I fell in love with the country first in 2006.

I was enamored with its environment, tropical warm air, and 85-degree, crystal-clear water. The monkeys, the sloths, and even that yellow pit viper who was sleeping on a tree branch all made my heart skip a beat and my stomach flutter.

Those memories never left me.

Everything was so green, vibrant, and alive. The energy swept me up and I too was vibrant and alive, surrounded by life.

Wild. Wholehearted. Life.

I wanted to bathe in that feeling, every day, every moment, every breath. My attempts to recapture it upon returning home were never the same. Mainly, I couldn't physically breathe. I was so sick in California.

It's hard to have an epic romance with life when you're allergic to the climate you call home.

I would find myself sniffling through the seasons, with red, watery eyes and ear infections, unable to fully appreciate the beauty around me.

But even though I'm adventurous and had strong motivation to leave California, I've never been the type of person who could spontaneously fill a backpack and move out of the country. I spent four years planning and thinking of ways to get myself down here.

The adventure truly began in 2012 when Harmony, my 17-year-old cat, and I got through security at San Francisco Airport and finally sat down in the first-class cabin. I couldn't stop smiling and the pre-flight champagne was certainly a nice little bonus in celebrating the momentous occasion.

Unfortunately, keeping a cat in a carrier for 20 hours is not an ideal situation and Harmony did not share my enthusiasm for the new life that lay ahead of us. Around 12:30 a.m. we experienced turbulence, sending him into what can only be described as a kitty panic attack. He was literally trying to push his way out of his carrier.

It took me 90 minutes to calm him down (he has quite a set of lungs on him). This did not help his mental state (or mine) and the merry-making effects of the champagne had long since expired.

At the Admiral's Club in Miami, I used one of the showers to give him time to stretch and eat, not that he was interested. Nor did I realize that this would be my last "normal" shower for a very long time.

We eventually arrived safe and sound in Liberia. I stepped off the plane and could actually take a deep breath in, feeling the humid air enter my lungs and the moist heat grace my dry skin. If lungs could dance, mine would've been doing the tango (or maybe the Merengue since that takes a little less coordination). I knew from that moment on... my skin would never need moisturizer, my lips wouldn't be cracked and bleeding and I would be able to breathe. No matter what I faced in the days, months and years ahead, the baseline improvements to my health would give me a happiness that would carry me through the rough days.

Our trip through customs was less challenging than it could have been. They didn't even look at Harmony but did give me a hard time about having ten bags of luggage. Eventually they gave up, perhaps when they realized I was not going to pay them off...

On previous trips, the drivers commissioned to collect me at the airport had run late or failed to show up at all, but my sun-kissed new life allowed for our private shuttle driver to be there right on schedule. An hour later, we found ourselves on the bumpy dirt road leading to Langosta (another trauma for my poor cat) and our driver dropped us off at our new home in Tamarindo.

Our life on the Rich Coast had commenced.

The First 100 Days

The first house I lived in was exactly what I imagined it would be and I loved it. There was a nice kitchen with concrete countertops, painted blue (making it very clear that I was in Central America now), and it even had a little stove and oven. While larger than a toaster oven, it was still quite small (which my friends told me was actually large by Costa Rican standards), and so I called it my Easy Bake Oven.

As I'd come to find out, ovens are not commonplace in Costa Rica. A *tica* friend (native Costa Rican) once told me that *ticos* didn't bake and she didn't think they even knew how. Having traveled outside of Costa Rica, she always complained about how dreadful the bread was in Costa Rican bakeries. And she's right. It's horrible.

But I digress... back to my house. The upstairs was just a one-room A-frame loft with a large picture window on one side and a sliding glass door on the other. It opened to a breathtaking view of a *zona verde* (green zone). The stairs to get up to the loft were a little wacky and Harmony wouldn't even attempt them for the first two weeks. Eventually though, we both figured out how to maneuver them. Slowly. Having fallen twice the previous year and basically fracturing my tailbone, I couldn't take any chances now that I was living in a foreign country with no health insurance!

There were no cabinets or closets in the entire house. Not a single one, not even in the kitchen. Everything was just... open. It was definitely an adjustment; I like things to be clean and organized. (And to be able to shove miscellaneous items into a closet or drawer that I don't want others to see!) As I would come to find out, it's common in *tico* homes to not have closets, drawers or cabinets - something that I still miss desperately today.

The downstairs had a tiny little bathroom, about 6 feet x 6 feet, with a standing shower, a pedestal sink, and two small shelves to house toiletries. There was no medicine cabinet.

The backyard was huge with a covered patio and a place to dry my laundry. There was no dryer but there was a full-sized washing machine outside.

It wasn't a mansion or one of the eco-retreats I'd stayed at while vacationing, but it was my home and I knew we'd make it work despite the absence of good places to hide my various odds and ends.

Even though I was 200 meters from the beach, I could still hear the waves crashing on the shore, especially at night when it was high tide. After the crickets quieted down, the waves would lull me to sleep.

One early morning I was hanging my laundry outside when I heard the sound of leaves rustling above me. A big troop of howlers were passing through. I stopped what I was doing, just to enjoy the moment and realized, I was home.

Living next to the *zona verde* was like being in a live version of "*Where's Waldo*". It was so amazing how much I could see, just from sitting in my "outdoor office". Admittedly, it could be rather distracting. Every time I heard the hum of a hummingbird, a breaking branch from a monkey or an iguana (during the day) or raccoon (during the night) jumping on my patio roof from the trees, I would look up to see if I could find where the sound was coming from and who was creating it.

I had to force myself not to bring my camera outside with me when working as it often became like an episode of Alice in Wonderland. I would end up following whatever caught my eye and would spend hours immersing myself in the natural world.

When I was on vacation, that was a great thing. But, actually living here, there was always work to be done, and as much as I'd like to, I can't go following white rabbits down holes (or now, I'd say agoutis – which are like brown rabbits but they actually look more like huge rats).

In the first month, here's what I saw from my kitchen, my hammock, my bedroom and the pool...

- Hundreds of dragonflies and butterflies
- So many species of colorful and sweet sounding birds
- Monkeys
- Halloween crabs
- Garrobos
- Centipedes (or millipedes? I don't know how to tell the difference! All I know is it had a lot of tiny legs)
- Caterpillars
- Raccoons

And of course, those things that you don't really want to see: spiders, termites, wasps, scorpions, beetles and ants. There were lots of ants and termites. The ants in particular were so bizarre. Every morning, there were about 15 of them on my kitchen counter... sleeping. No joke. They weren't dead. They were asleep. I guess they got tired of trying to look for food. And the termites were interesting to watch. They build these strange tunnels outside that seem to go nowhere. And they're much larger than I imagined. Of course, as I've said before in previous books, all insects are bigger here in the tropics.

From the time the howlers and birds woke me up in the morning, and I could look out my sliding glass door in my bedroom (which had no curtains), I was seeing nature exist, change, be. I even got a video one morning of a halloween crab eating a centipede! Unfortunately, one of the halloween crabs fell into the pool. And they're land crabs, not water crabs, so by the time I found him, he was already gone.

It took Harmony a while but he eventually figured out that this new hot and humid environment was now home. Going from the California desert to tropical Costa Rica was a big adjustment. I wondered what he thought about the haunting sounds of the howlers every morning and evening, or the high-pitched chirping of the geckos that live in the house. Surprisingly, he had little interest in the bugs - there were so many geckos and tiny baby crabs but he walked right past them and showed no interest. He did see a *garrobo* (iguana) outside one day and that interested him, but once it disappeared around the corner, Harmony's interest disappeared as well.

Another amazing thing was that, other than Harmony's extreme thirst, which I hoped was due to the heat and not his kidneys failing again, his health was really good in those early days.

A few months before we left, his vet told me that half of his larynx was paralyzed and it would never get better. He would have these awful violent attacks every time he tried to purr. And the vets said it would get worse if I brought him to a location where the weather was hot. I thought I was going to have to let him go just before the move, but somehow in those last few weeks my little miracle cat, who seems to have more than 9 lives, cured himself and he had no problems upon arrival. He wasn't eating very much, but he was 17 and it was hot, so I figured he wasn't that hungry. Other than that, he seemed totally healthy and happy. And he knew that we were home because he started defending his territory. When other cats would come around, he'd crouch down low and hiss angrily if they tried to get on his turf.

Aside from Harmony and I getting to know the local creatures, there was lots to do to make our new life comfortable and turn our little casita into a home. Though as I started to do the things that locals do, I also started to see the challenges and frustrations that would become constants in my life here.

Knowing that theft was rampant in Tamarindo, I rented a car on one of my first days here and drove to Santa Cruz to buy a safe. The store didn't have any at the time but told me to come back the following week.

That was really my first experience of the concept of Mañana.

Renting a car was not cheap or easy. But as I would come to learn, there are only a few shops around that carry certain goods, and they don't always have what you need when you need it. It kind of reminds me of Price Club (now Costco) 20+ years ago. I remember going there and often times, they wouldn't have the same items that they had the week or month prior.

That's kind of what every store in Costa Rica is like.

One of the most important things I learned these early days was that I always have to do the laundry first thing in the morning so it will dry before the rain comes. This was an easy lesson to learn one day as I was working in my hammock and it started to rain. The drying line was only a few feet behind me but being in the hammock, I have a tendency to get into somewhat of a blissful state, ignoring what's happening around me.

Fortunately, my housekeeper ran outside to remind me "*las ropas!*" and saved the clothes from the downpour.

I was working hard to practice my Spanish and picking up quite a lot. While I would talk with most of my friends in English (as most of them were either expats from the US or from European countries), I was talking in Spanish with people at the bank, the grocery store, the pharmacy, the veterinarian. I often didn't understand much of what was said but I got the gist, nodding my head often as if I completely understood everything. However, that sometimes made them talk faster, and I'd then have to stop them and ask that they speak slower.

Taxi drivers always presented a good opportunity for speaking Spanish. Although with them, it was always the same conversation. They'd ask me where I was from, if I was married, if I had children, if I liked to go out, if I danced. That was pretty much every conversation with every taxi driver. It kind of became amusing. Sort of. A tad annoying as well.

At the two-month mark, I wrote this blog, while still in the honeymoon phase of my arrival in Costa Rica:

LOST AND FOUND IN THE LAND OF MAÑANA

Well, I'm at the two-month mark now. It's still surreal. Here are the top reasons why I moved to Costa Rica (I could have probably listed 100+ reasons but I figured I had to stop at some point):

1. *Warm, tropical weather year-round, and no threat of hurricanes;*
2. *Friendly, helpful, and beautiful people, inside and out;*
3. *Simpler lifestyle - less cars, less traffic, more walkable, more sense of community;*
4. *Awesome environment and environmental protections (over 25% of the land is protected and much of the unprotected land remains undeveloped);*
5. *Less pollution;*
6. *Locally grown, fresh food;*
7. *No army since 1948 and no nuclear power (and they actually plan to be carbon neutral by 2021);*
8. *No allergies to the food or the local environment;*
9. *Democratic country with a female president;*
10. *Cost of living is greatly reduced compared to California;*
11. *No chapped lips;*
12. *No stop lights for approximately 70 kilometers from the town where I'm living (well, there is one in Santa Cruz but it's pretty rinky-dink and it seems like a lot of people don't even pay attention to what color the light is!);*
13. *A local airport and an international airport close by;*

14. *San Jose is less than an hour flight from the local airport;*
15. *No quarantine for bringing pets into the country;*
16. *Fresh mangoes at $0.70 each;*
17. *All the gallo pinto and lizano that I could possibly want;*
18. *I feel fully alive, radiant, and purposeful here;*
19. *I get to try surfing and stand-up-paddling again and hopefully will make one of them a daily practice;*
20. *I'm already in paradise so every day feels like being on holiday;*
21. *There's no such thing as a heater here in Guanacaste;*
22. *I have more opportunity to explore areas of the country that I haven't yet visited;*
23. *My wardrobe consists of sundresses and sandals;*
24. *My feet receive a daily exfoliation from walking on the beach;*
25. *Pura Vida!*

Now, many years later, much of the above still holds true. Not all, but a lot of it. And besides being healthy, it's for these reasons (and many more) that I choose to stay and call this place *Home*.

On my first 90-day visa run out of the country, I stayed at Jicaro Island Ecolodge in Nicaragua and a strange feeling came over me. I realized that the last time I was at Jicaro, I made the comment (to the universe - no one else was around) that the *casitas* at Jicaro would be the perfect place to live.

That if only it had a small kitchen, I could easily live in this *casita* full time.

As I sat there, looking around, I realized my little *tipica* house in Costa Rica had almost all of the same elements that the Jicaro *casitas* have. Of course, Jicaro is a 5-star eco-lodge and the *casitas* are stunning, and my new little home was far from perfect but both are two-story, wooden houses. The ceiling in the living room is wood, which makes up the floor of my bedroom. Most of the Jicaro *casita* has floor-to-ceiling windows, just like my house, and both are surrounded by trees.

Also, like my house, the windows downstairs that look out to the patio don't have any curtains or window coverings. Both patios have a hammock and awning. The master bedroom is the only room upstairs in both places and both are very simple. They both even have wood shelves instead of dressers. The roofs are made of aluminum and the interior second floor ceilings are made of wood. In both places, I can hear howlers in the morning and birds chirping throughout the day.

A friend once reminded me that when I want something, to "ask, ask, ask". My little Tamarindo *casita* was proof that the universe provides when you do just that.

In addition to my trip to Jicaro, I did some other traveling within Costa Rica in those first 100 days. What I'd come to learn is that I felt most in "reality" when I was traveling. Which was hard to explain at the time until I realized that Tamarindo was kind of like fantasyland. And for me, that wasn't a good thing. You may hear me say this several times...I'm a realist. I like real people, real food, real authentic living.

But despite the oddities of my new life, the first 100 days were good. I was shedding excess pounds that I had brought with me from California, working on my tan, settling in and learning the ins and outs of what it takes to live in a foreign country. One of my favorite things to do was to wake up every morning between 5:00 a.m. and 5:30 a.m. to head down to the beach in my flip flops, and take a walk along the sandy shore as the sun came up. I was adjusting happily to my newfound healthy life.

Chapter 2
Learning to Grocery Shop and Cook All Over Again

"There is no end to education. It is not that you read a book, pass an examination, and finish with education. The whole of life, from the moment you are born to the moment you die, is a process of learning."

Krishnamurti

I accomplished quite a lot in those first 100 days. I opened a bank account (although it took me 30 of the 100 days to do so), and shockingly, learned how much food actually costs when you're living in a country where everything is imported. Something I just hadn't thought of when I was vacationing here!

Going to the grocery store here often times gives me a headache.

The Automercado (Costa Rica's closest version to a Whole Foods) because it's so darn expensive, and then the local markets because they tend to be so disorganized and lacking so many items that I need. I did eventually get used to going to 3 different stores to find products but there seems to be no rhyme or reason to the layout in any of them or what they carry on a regular basis.

For example, in one supermarket, the flour is next to the Top Ramen and the Chinese food. And the tortillas are next to the jam, *dulce de leche*, and chocolate sauce. It boggles my mind as to how they created the store and what they were thinking when they did it or how they restock. I needed baking soda but all they had was baking powder. Two different brands of powder and like 15 bottles! But no soda.

With my iPhone I quickly Googled substitutes for baking soda. My choices were to triple the powder, or mix the powder and cream of tartar together. You want to guess which one I ended up with? Only baking powder because there was no cream of tartar. Tartar sauce, yes. Cream of tartar, no. And it seems so odd that they don't have baking soda but they have tahini. I needed the tahini to make hummus so I was happy to find it, but still odd.

I had also yet to learn that yellow lemons didn't exist. Contrary to popular belief here, there is a difference between limes and lemons. Limon refers to both types. But they're totally different. Like, you put a green limon into a bottle of Corona, you put a yellow limon into hummus. But it would be months before I'd see any yellow lemons and when they finally arrived at Automercado, they were more than a dollar a piece and only there for a few weeks.

There were some other things that also surprised me. Like the eggs aren't refrigerated. They're not even near a refrigeration unit.

One day, as I was checking out, I asked the cashier, *"isn't it necessary to keep eggs cold?"* She smiled and laughed a little, and replied, *"No, not necessary."* I truly believe eggs should be refrigerated but (thanks to Google) I would come to learn that the US refrigerates its eggs because of some cleaning process they go through before arriving in the stores. No such cleaning process exists in Costa Rica. Which you can easily tell, since there's often times feathers, and other miscellaneous things we don't like to think about, still on them. I also found it odd that some of the egg sellers sold their eggs by weight, not quantity.

You can also just buy one egg, if that's all you need.

When I shopped at the Automercado, I would get perplexing looks from the cashiers when I would spend $200-300 on one trip. For them, that's probably a little less than half their monthly paycheck. But I didn't want to succumb to only eating rice and beans. I finally had the time and energy to cook, only now it was incredibly expensive and also extremely difficult to find many foods I was used to. Some products just don't exist here!

The Automercado has more of what I look for and a better selection, but it's the most expensive grocery store here. However, they do seem to have a nicer selection of fresh fruits and vegetables plus more variety. They also carry garbanzo beans and sundried tomatoes so I can make hummus (the other markets did not), and they even have Kashi cereal and Back to Nature products. But like I said, that all comes at a really high price.

I would dream of someone sending me either Skippy Peanut Butter or Trader Joe's Crunchy Almond Butter (they only have Jif here and I've always been a Skippy girl). Oh, and that good trail mix from Trader Joe's that has the chocolate chips, almonds, peanuts, cranberries and butterscotch chips. And a case of almond or soy milk. I bet that with the number of expats living in Tamarindo, if they were to open a Trader Joe's here, it could potentially be their best-selling store.

A year into living in Costa Rica, I moved from Tamarindo to Quepos and I met Emilio, the owner of the Mini Price Store, who goes to PriceMart (the Costa Rica version of Costco) weekly and brings back all the products that those of us without cars (or a desire to ever visit San Jose) can then buy at a slightly higher price. He's kind of like a present from the universe for me. Mini Price (or as I call it, *my little Costco*) is where I find the kalamata olives, quinoa, tofu and the Downy softener. So I suck it up and pay the inflated prices with a smile.

Apples are special treats that I give myself on occasion. Whereas mangoes only cost $0.75, an apple will cost upwards of $1.50. And often-times, they're already soft and mealy inside. But they still make for great juice, when I have enough money to actually buy a few.

Kalamata olives are often difficult to find (or they're around but by the time I get to MiniPrice, someone has already bought all the bottles). And they're expensive at $18 for a 6-ounce bottle. I started going to MaxiPali (which is owned by Wal Mart) more frequently as it's the only place I've been able to find coconut water for my morning smoothies. I still find it so strange that coconut water is hard to find here despite all the ACTUAL coconuts. They also carry ground flax seeds, something I haven't found anywhere else in town.

Back in 2013, I was desperately searching for chia seeds and couldn't find them anywhere...until one special day I came across 4 bags! And knowing that things like this are not often found here, I decided to buy two, doing my best to not be greedy and take all four. However, when I went to check out, the cashier told me they weren't in the system so I couldn't buy them at all!

Now, normally in a situation like that, they'll simply say, "Ah, it's probably $5, how does that sound?" But not that day...

I desperately wanted the chia seeds so I asked to speak with the manager. There had to be a price! It was on the shelf after all! One of the clerks took me upstairs to meet with the owner. It was a family-owned store and I met with the owner's daughter. She explained to me that the chia was for her family and wasn't supposed to be put on the shelf, hence why there wasn't a price tag. But she wanted to do something nice so she offered to sell me one for $5. And I told her that if she could get her supplier to bring more, I'd buy lots. Unfortunately, that market closed a few weeks later and I was once again without chia.

Until...one day a few months later I was walking through the *feria* (farmer's market) and heard a vendor calling out *"Chia! Chia!"* Oh, what a special day that was. He had several large (and expensive) bags of chia for sale. The *feria* is also where I find kale. For my first year in Quepos, the only farmer to grow this dark leafy green was Gilberth who, like Emilio, I have a deep gratitude for because they provide me with a sense of home. Just a little bit of normalcy in this crazy backwards land.

On one particular day when I arrived at Gilberth's table, I learned that all of the kale had been bought, however I happened to go to another farmer's booth and found kale there as well.

Supply and demand, my friends. Or maybe it was the universe. Gilberth promised to set aside a few bunches for me the following week, which was so very kind.

The *feria* is where I buy fruits and vegetables that are out of the norm. Sometimes, for fun, I take things home even though I have no idea what they are. Water apples (looks like a pear, tastes like a watered down apple), and *mamon chinos* (a type of lychee) are two of my favorites as they're both super refreshing on hot days. Unfortunately, they're seasonal and while we have year-round summer here, many fruits will only be found for a few months (so I embrace the impermanence and fully enjoy them while they last).

The *feria* is also where I can sometimes track down hard-to-find products like Himalayan sea salt, cacao, freshly dried herbs and spices, and even fresh sugar cane. I've never actually bought the sugar cane but it's fun to watch it go through the machine and be pressed into actual sugar.

At the supermarkets, I've learned to be careful with the spices, always reading the labels prior to buying. My ex once brought home "complete seasoning" which had, as its first ingredient, "MSG". As soon as he left, it was thrown in the trash. I could've given it to one of my *tica* neighbors or my housekeeper (as I'm sure they would probably use it), but I prefer not to perpetuate such a negative food energy. I also always look at the expiration dates. So often the date on the item will already be expired!

A few months in to living here, I was really getting into cooking. But I was still running into problems. I couldn't find items like:

- Chickpea flour
- Maca
- Goji berries
- Cashews
- Agave Syrup
- Coconut oil
- Graham crackers

I find all these great, healthy, vegan, and oftentimes gluten-free recipes, but can't actually make any of them because of a lack of ingredients available at the stores. I wanted to make chickpea flatbread with rosemary. I figured... I have chickpeas, I have rosemary, so what could be the problem? Oh yes, I need a coffee or spice grinder to make the chickpea flour because I can't buy it here. I might be able to find a coffee grinder...somewhere. But "where" is the key word.

And yes, in 2012, before moving to Quepos and having access to my little Costco, even cashews were on that list of unattainable items. It seems crazy to me that I couldn't find them and I sometimes felt like I'm losing my mind as I was searching through the tiny snack bags of walnuts, pecans and almonds on the grocery store shelves. I mean really – how do cashews not exist here? I've always wanted to make cashew cheese and once again, I now had the time but not the ingredient. *Sigh*

LOST AND FOUND IN THE LAND OF MAÑANA

Do you know I can't even buy coconut oil at the Automercado? It doesn't exist! Like the water! I'm sure it's all being exported to the US but still, can't we have a few bottles here? So many of my recipes call for it and it's crazy that in a country that produces massive amounts of coconuts, my only oil options are Canola, Olive and Crisco. Every once in a while, I can find sesame. And you better believe I buy it when I see it! I just don't look at the price.

But...to find the limeade in the lime...I can buy contraband Cuban products here. ;)

I'll admit that these days I become a little greedy when I go to the store and find bags of quinoa (2 cups dry for $10). I often buy things not because I need them in that moment, but because I don't know when I'll ever find them again in the future. I'll buy them all and then store them in my tiny freezer (because of the humidity and the awful black bugs plus the cockroaches and ants, everything gets stored in the freezer). I do have a moment of hesitation when I'm putting the entire stock of quinoa into my shopping basket, knowing that I should only buy what I need and leave the rest for others to enjoy...but I can't risk not being able to find the quinoa (or kalamata olives or tofu or seaweed) again.

I've had people tell me that when they vacation here they bring their own food. One couple even said they bring butter from the States (they freeze it the night before their flight) as they don't like the butter options in the supermarkets - the butter here is white, in contrast to the yellow butter that we have in the US. Milk comes in boxes and is often not refrigerated. Other foods like refried beans, mayo and ketchup all come in these strange plastic bags. After having bought a few canned items (to keep on hand for an emergency), I now understand the plastic bags might be necessary, because with the tropical climate here, the cans I bought were all rusted after having sat in my kitchen for a few months.

It's incredibly difficult to find quality cereal here (unless you're at the Automercado). And when you do, it'll cost you upwards of $10/box. You can, however, find lots of poor quality, sugar-filled cereals.

The *pulperia* or little local supermarket is where most of the *ticos* shop. Pali and MaxiPali are owned by Walmart but there's never anything I want to buy from Pali (they don't even sell peanut butter!) and MaxiPali is outside of town and requires a taxi ,which doesn't balance out for the cost of the cheaper products there. But they do have the coconut water. The local supermarkets and *pulperias* are usually small - three to four times smaller than a 7-Eleven. And the "supers" are actually supermarkets so it's just astonishing how very little food they carry.

At the pulperias, you'll usually only find the commonly eaten staples (i.e. the most commonly used foods in the traditional *gallo pinto* breakfast and *casado* eaten for lunch and dinner):

- Beans
- Rice

- Flour
- Corn flour
- Bananas (which are often black as there's no a/c in these buildings), onions, tomatoes, red peppers, cucumbers, plantains, yucca and potatoes
- Turrialba cheese (really bad cheese unless you buy it in Turrialba, freshly made)
- Eggs, chicken, and pork/sausage
- Soda, chips, and candy (but their chips and candy are just weird, not worth the calories)
- Bread and tortillas
- Top Ramen style soups
- There might be a few small items like Kleenex and toilet paper but that's really the extent. Sometimes there isn't even that.

And most of that food is a whole load of starch, not very healthy, nor a complete meal, definitely not green but at times, when I lived near them, I'd pop in there to buy something small as the walk to MiniPrice was much further.

However, trying to see it from the *ticos'* perspective, that's really all they need: eggs, rice and beans, some corn flour to make tortillas, a few plantains, cheese to have as a side to *gallo pinto* at breakfast, and chicken and more rice and beans for lunch and dinner. And then maybe a bag of pork rinds as a snack (which my *tico* friends tried to tell me were not actually made from pork...read the labels people!).

There are some stores that only sell individual products, like the butcher shops, bread shops, and pharmacies (where you buy makeup and other toiletries – don't try to find these items in a *super*). You'll also see vendors parked on the side of the road selling fruits and vegetables out of the truck bed or even the trunk of their car. In Quepos, there's also a flower shop and many, many hardware stores. Very European, I suppose. Okay, I don't actually remember there being that many hardware stores in Europe, but there's literally one on every corner here. Hardware stores here are like wine shops in Italy. There are also a lot more tiny supermarkets dispersed around the town, and lots of shops that only sell vegetables and fruit. Which seems odd since *ticos* actually eat very few veggies.

I was excited to see bread shops in Quepos as the bread in the supermarkets is dreadful. But I was sad to find out that my local *tica* friend was right when she told me that the bread here, whether bought in a supermarket or freshly made by a baker, is abysmal. Just like the cheese. And any other pastries. At the markets, you usually won't find sourdough bread, bagels, english muffins, or donuts, and if you do, they'll either be stale or poorly made. Bagels at the markets are known to taste like hockey pucks. Having such dreadful options for bread and cheese does make it easier to be vegan, at least when it comes to cravings and temptations!

One of my favorite treats, dates, are also very difficult to find here. I was told that the large

"Costco-like" store only carries them during the holidays as a special treat for the *ticos*. The Automercado usually has them but again, the Automercado is both expensive and now, over an hour away. Without a car, it becomes a gigantic hassle. When I do manage to get there, I usually buy out their entire stock of dates and store them in the freezer (with everything else).

Wine is also a tragic tale - one that makes me nearly cry whenever I think about it. First, you'll pay three to four times the amount you'd pay in the US and most of the wines are from South America. Second, most of them are awful. Having worked harvest for a winery selling $100 bottles of wine, it's truly a sad day when I go to my liquor store and have to spend $25 on a bottle that would have cost $7 in the US. And then because it really is just a $7 bottle of wine, it isn't the quality that I'm accustomed to or want.

A friend tried to convince me to buy the box wine, and for quite a while I held out as it wasn't a road I was prepared to go down. Going from $100 bottles of wine to box wine is a drastic change – but one that eventually, I made. And trust me, I have a certificate in wine studies from University of California, Irvine, and there *is* a difference between a $7 bottle and a $100 bottle.

You can also find wine in some of the *pulperias*, which truly frightens me. Because the *pulperias* are not air conditioned and rarely do they have the fans on, so the wine is just sitting out in 90+ degree temperatures. It makes me shudder to think about it.

I do, at times, choose traditional Costa Rican foods. I actually like *gallo pinto* immensely (mixed rice and beans served with eggs for breakfast) and I'll treat myself to it every once in a while, but there's too much starch in the meal to make it a worthwhile and healthy dish to eat on a regular basis. When I make it at home, I always use brown rice. Brown rice is more expensive but it's also far superior to white rice. White rice has absolutely no nutritional value. None.

One time I was shopping at the supermarket with an ex-boyfriend and he was buying items to make *gallo pinto*. He picked up a bag of white rice and I tried to explain to him that I'd prefer we buy the brown as it actually has some nutritional value. He proceeded to tell me: *"Chris, there's no difference, plus it's cheaper."* I had learned by that point not to argue with him over things like that - he wouldn't believe me even if I pointed out the nutritional value chart on each bag.

On cooking black beans and opening coconuts...

It's so easy, Chrissy!"

That's what people kept telling me when I asked them how to prepare dry black beans. As much as I tried to eat fresh and healthy in California, I admit that I cheated a lot when it came to preparing food, just based on the fact that I didn't have the hours in the day. And so I ate a lot of black beans from cans purchased at Trader Joes. Give me a little credit though – I did actually know that the dried beans were hard and something needed to be done with them. I just wasn't sure what.

So, since I really wasn't getting any solid answers from my local friends, I did what any 21st century girl would do...I Googled it. But even with Googling, I was left with many unanswered questions. So I used several different websites to piece it all together and *voila*! I made my first batch of black beans.

I'm sure my housekeeper came in and wondered why my stovetop turned black. But I'm proud of myself for finally getting around to slow cooking and enjoying every moment along the way. And I have to admit – fresh black beans are a lot better tasting than canned. Same goes for chickpeas (in case you were wondering).

One day early on I was in the grocery store and saw coconuts. I didn't purchase one at the time but I kept thinking about it and so the next time I went, I bought one. Now, like the beans, I had no idea how to even open the coconut much less cook with it. But I bought it ($1.00 each), brought it home, put it on my cutting board and stared at it for a while. I picked it up, took a closer look, shook it, and then took my very sharp knife and attempted to cut into it but... realized I'd probably lose a finger doing that. So I went back to Google.

From what I read, it seemed like I was going to need some non-kitchen equipment to get this fruit open, so I found my Ziploc bag that holds the tools I brought from the States. I started with a screwdriver but didn't get very far. Then I pulled out my wine opener, thinking maybe I could twist my way into it – at least to get the water out of it. That actually got me into the coconut. From here, I dumped out the water into a Pyrex.

The instructions I found then said to take a very sharp knife and cut along its equator and after a few turns, it would just break open. Yeah...no. That didn't happen and again, I was concerned about keeping all of my fingers.

Another option was to put the coconut into a plastic bag and hit it with a hammer against concrete.

So I grabbed a hammer, a plastic bag and went outside. The top flew off but I don't think that was the "equator". From here though, I was able to take a knife and scoop out the meat. Although there wasn't much of it. Admittedly, I got a small coconut. I'm smart enough to know that starting small is a lot better than getting the biggest one and losing a finger or two.

Then, I took a sip of the water – it was refreshingly delicious. So much different than the boxes of "fresh coconut water" that you can buy in the stores in the States (sorry friends, that's not fresh coconut). Of course, I had no idea what to do with the meat. I tried to shred it using a grater but the pieces were too small and soft to grate. One of my cookbooks recommended mixing it with rice and lime so I went with that and made a black bean soup to accompany it.

Both turned out okay. Although I wished I had brought my immersion blender from California for the soup. I also used a little too much lime in the rice so it was extra tangy.

You see, I don't actually follow recipes...I read what the ingredients are and then do what I want with the measurements. As long as you accept whatever the results may be, experimenting can be fun, right? But overall, the mix of brown rice, lime and coconut was quite pleasing and aromatic.

Side note...here in Costa Rica, they call coconuts "*pipa*".

They seem to have an affectionate term for everything. So if you happen to hear someone yelling out: *Pipa! Pipa!* Go find the man (I say man as I've never actually seen a woman selling coconuts) and ask him for a fresh, cold *pipa*. It shouldn't cost you more than 500 *colones*. (About $1). Although I did once have a man try to charge me C1,250 – that there is the "blue-eyed tax". I called him on it and walked away.

Choosing Compassionate Eating in The Land of Pork Rinds

When I first arrived in Tamarindo, I became a vegetarian again, (after being 99% vegan in California), because it was just too difficult to find certain foods. As I settled into my new life I wanted to return to a fully compassionate and more mindful eating practice so my first step was to find ways to be vegan that did not break the bank. Yes, there were more vegan options at Automercado, but the expense was what was killing my budget. Not something I could do on a regular basis!

And I *so* love making healthy versions of baked goods. Mini mango muffins are one of my favorites. I used to post pictures on Facebook with text that said something like: *"Mango muffins at Casa Chrissy today! Stop by and pick up a few!"* However, I stopped doing that when I found out that people thought I was selling weed-filled muffins.

Seriously. I really want to make this clear...food can be magic without it containing weed.

I love feeding people. I find it nourishes my spirit to prepare compassionate meals for others, but here in Costa Rica, there are three problems I came up against trying to share food with people here:

1. People will flake on you;
2. They are wary of vegan food; and
3. They think you're putting weed into it
   (and are disappointed when you're not).

Moving from Tamarindo to the larger town of Quepos, I've found that it's much easier to be mostly vegan and I'm now again what I would call a vegetarian with vegan tendencies. Out of respect for vegans, I don't want to say I'm full-on vegan as there are times when I have very few choices and will eat something with eggs or cheese. But it's rare.

What's probably more difficult than the limited food choices, however, is the stigma that vegetarianism has here. First, most of the *ticos* just don't get it (except for vegetarian ones!). They think that you'll still eat anything but cows. So fish, pigs, chickens, etc...all okay. Countless times I've ordered a *casado* (their typical lunch), specifically requested vegetarian, and received chicken on the plate.

Second, it's still not widely accepted by the *gringos* here either. You'd think they'd have a more open mind, having had the fortitude to do something different and move to a foreign country. But no – many of them are as close-minded as the Ticos about people who are vegetarian and brazenly make jokes at my expense.

I'm often told: *"We didn't invite you because we didn't think there'd be any food options for you."* And they're probably right. But there's always something – even if it's just rice and beans.

There was one time that my *tico* team member and I were traveling and staying at a hotel where they had a vegetarian tofu dish. It was encrusted in macadamia nuts. I offered some of it to him to try.

Because tofu is pretty much an unknown food item here, he was open to the idea and liked it - so much so that he finished it off for me. He had no idea of the stigma associated with tofu and wouldn't you know it, it's something he said he'd have again. Had I offered it to a *gringo* who was well aware of the stigma, their reaction would probably have been different and they probably wouldn't have even tried it.

It's sad how much people miss out on because of silly preconceptions.

Another time I made kale chips for a *tico* friend who was visiting. He looked at them strangely at first (dark, green and a vegetable – how could these possibly taste good?), but then realized once he tried them that they were actually very good. Since then, I've made them for others - both *gringos* and *ticos* - and while I received the same disgusted look, all were surprisingly happy when they tentatively bit into the chip.

Little by little. *Poco a poco*...we will move away from the pork rinds and to healthier and more compassionate foods.

I was eating lunch with a friend one day when she started to question my desire to be vegan, especially in a country like Costa Rica which is not exactly vegan friendly. She said, *"You're only one person - what difference does it make?"*

The truth is. it makes a big difference to me. It makes a difference to how I feel about myself and my place in the world. It makes a difference when I share my compassionate meals with others, and they enjoy them, feel fulfilled, and talk to others about how delicious my vegan food was. They may not become vegan or vegetarian but by sharing my beliefs with others in a mindful way, it allows their minds to become more open. It creates a positive ripple effect. It allows stereotypes of bad or not nourishing vegan food to be diminished.

It provides an opportunity to teach others that there is more than one way to live one's life.
And that makes all the difference...

Chapter 3
Making Friends With The Creepy Crawlies

"If we were to wipe out insects alone on this planet, the rest of life and humanity with it would mostly disappear from the land. Within a few months."

E. O. Wilson

Since Day One here in Costa Rica, I've learned that I have to live with ants. And other creepy crawlies. It's just a part of daily life.

I no longer kill the ants. I've learned that it's honestly not worth the effort (or the paper towel usage). They keep coming back, as do the spiders, cockroaches and unfortunately, the occasional scorpion. I'm actually okay with spiders, snakes, scorpions and other scary wildlife...as long as they stay outside. My home is my sanctuary. And they are not invited in. On the off chance that one does find its way inside, then I do everything I can to safely remove it and return it to its home. Usually.

Scorpions are a major threat (while not deadly, I'd prefer not to be stung or have my cats stung) so although they're fast, if I can catch up to them, they usually don't live very long. I've rescued a few but have found it's just easier to kill them. And then I say a prayer that karma understands that I'm protecting my fur babies and doesn't come after me. Not having a car puts me in a predicament of being a mindful mama and ensuring my cats are always taken care of, which often means killing creepy crawlies to protect them. And... even if there was an emergency vet hospital (which there isn't), I wouldn't have a car to get my cats to it!

The cockroaches are another creepy-crawly that don't last long in my house. Now, with the cats, Lluvia (one of my newly adopted fur babies in 2014) is actually the killer. She waits for them every night and will usually kill a few a week. I want to be clear here – I have a clean home. I even have a housekeeper who cleans twice a week! But roaches are a never-ending problem in the tropics and I can't seem to get rid of them. I'm grateful for Lluvia, but I do wish she'd stop bringing the half-dead roaches to my bed in the middle of the night. Not a pleasant way to wake up.

The geckos, I don't have a problem with, inside or outside my house. Other than their poop. I was told that their poop is actually poisonous if ingested which my first thought was: *mouth breathers beware when you're sleeping.* Upon further research though, it seems the person who told me that was incorrect. That being said, it's still probably best to clean it up as quickly as possible. They poop everywhere by the way. And while I like the baby geckos because they're kind of cute, and you can literally see their little hearts beating as the skin is so thin and transparent (a nice reminder that we all live and breathe), they're not so precious when they get older...and bigger.

Now the monkeys - those are always a treat. At my house in Manuel Antonio, we had nearly daily visits from the endangered squirrel monkeys (*mono titis*) and the white-faced monkeys (*capuchins*). On occasion, I could hear a lone howler, but he isn't a part of a troop and didn't come around very often.

The only time I get frustrated with the monkeys is when I've got clean clothes, sheets, and towels hanging on the line outside and they decide the hanging items are a fun place to play...with their dirty little hands and feet. Forget about the natural jungle gym to their right, left, and behind my home... Chrissy's soft, clean sheets are way more fun to play with and sleep on.

They're such a delight to watch that frustrations of dirty hand prints generally dissipate pretty quickly.

There are also the frogs, butterflies, crickets, fireflies and dragonflies that find their way into my home who I have to help find their way out.

While Harmony didn't have much interest, my newly adopted cats have especially loved having them in the house – it's pure entertainment for them. The butterflies and dragonflies might be tough for them to catch but the frogs hopping around down on the ground are much easier. That's when you'll see me running around trying to catch it myself before they do! And let me tell you, frog catching is its own form of exercise. I will say that Sunshine (my other newly adopted fur baby) has become quite good at catching moths and flying termites. He then pops them into his mouth - it's quite the sight.

There was also one morning when I was woken up by the sound of a beetle hyperventilating under my bed at 3 a.m. The cats were under there too, staring at it, totally fascinated. It had flipped itself over (or perhaps the cats had flipped it over) and was literally hyperventilating. Loudly. I managed to get it from under the bed, away from the cats and into a safe place.

Creepy crawlies.... everywhere.

One day I posted the photo of a scorpion on my Facebook page, and two people - one from the States and one from Costa Rica - told me to plant lavender around the house because scorpions don't like it. So I went to the *vivero* (plant nursery).

Me: Do you have any lavender?

Rolando: No, maybe next month.

Me: Do you have any other plants that scorpions don't like?

Rolando (smiling now and kind of laughing...at me): No, nothing stops scorpions, including lavender.

Me: Now with a look of total panic

Rolando: Don't worry, scorpions are totally safe...unless you're allergic. Are you allergic to bees? Scorpions like to hang out on curtains, underneath pillows and really like wood – what is your house made of?

Me: I don't know, I haven't ever been stung by bees or scorpions! And my house is mostly wood!

Rolando: Well, don't worry, you'll be okay. It's the little scorpions that have the most venom and it's a lot more potent and fresh than the older scorpions' venom, which hurt less if they sting you. But what you have to worry about here is dengue.

Great. Dengue. A new problem to add to my growing list of things that are pretty much out of my control. So I hired Rolando to come to my house and spray for scorpions, and hopefully that might keep the mosquitoes and the resulting Dengue at bay as well. And maybe it will also help with the growing population of spiders in my house. I don't understand why they can't be outside – that's where their food is! Why do they like my home so much!?

I still look under my pillows every night, shake out my sheets, towels, and clothes, and am always mindful when I open and close the doors of my house to make sure no scorpions run inside or are hanging on the curtains.

The "scorpion spider" incident

Perhaps just like you, the first 30 minutes of the morning is usually a little bit of a haze for me. And on one particular morning this was no different. But as I turned on the water to wash my hands, something large, black, and scary ran out of the sink and up the wall in front of me.

Very quickly, I became fully awake.

That first house in Tamarindo seemed to be infested with spiders. The small ones I can handle and leave them alone. But the ones like that day... where I'm saying, "Oh _____ (fill in the blank)" multiple times are not okay in my house.

Because I practice the yoga principle of Ahimsa (non-harming), I first tried to assess the situation. Although, it being 5:30 a.m., my brain had to work a lot harder to think about what to do.

The largest mug I have still didn't have an opening wide enough for this scorpion spider's skinny, creepy legs (I came to learn that's what this heinous looking creature is called).

I admit, I did at one point consider whacking it with my shoe. It was way too big for a piece of tissue paper. And really, even if I did get it outside, there was no way of knowing if it wouldn't someday work its way back inside my house. So my shoe was still a viable option. But I decided to go with the large mug and the laminated pizza menu (gratitude to Esquina Pizzeria for the menu as it has saved many lives in my home).

I shooed it into a large area of the wall where I could place the mug over it, then slid the menu between the wall and the mug. It fought me though and made things so much more difficult. But I quickly ran out of the bathroom, through the kitchen and pushed the screen door open, dropping the menu from the mug onto the ground. The only problem was...no scorpion spider came out. I slowly turned the mug over and looked inside...no scorpion spider there either.

"Oh _____ (fill in the blank)". Now I'm jumping up and down but not seeing any spider fly off of me, and so I run back into the house, flip on all the lights and start searching the walls, curtains, floor, everywhere, to find this darned scorpion spider. Ten minutes I searched for that thing. Finally, I look behind the curtains and there it is, hanging out on the glass door.

Great, I can't whack it with my shoe now because with my luck, it will break the glass. So I get the mug again and this time, firmly hold the menu against the mug, kick the screen door open, and dump the spider out onto the ground.

The spider doesn't move. Perfect. I try to do good karma and I've killed it anyways. A few minutes later, I check back and see that it's moved a few feet, and I decide I'm going to help it move further away from my house so I shoo it into the dirt and said a little prayer for it to find a new home, far away from the interior of mine.

At that point, it was time for a cup of good Costa Rican coffee. In a different mug.

The *garrobo* in the pool incident

One day in my first house in Tamarindo, I was working at my kitchen table when I heard a *garrobo* (a black iguana) climb up the pool wall from the green zone behind it. They're not the most graceful creatures and tend to make quite a lot of noise. Within seconds, the giant lizard had jumped from the wall (which was about seven feet tall) into the pool, which was about five feet away. It made a huge splash, but as I looked out the glass windows of my kitchen, I couldn't see it.

I thought it might be swimming around, so I grabbed my camera thinking it would make a cool video. But it was at the bottom of the pool and not moving. I don't know how long it takes for a small creature like that to drown but I decided I should quickly assess the situation.

Here were my initial thoughts...

...The pool cleaners don't come again until Thursday. Which would mean I'd have a dead *garrobo* at the bottom of my pool for almost a week. That didn't sound pleasant and it would mean I couldn't go in the pool for that entire week, and considering my issue with germs, I'd have to make sure I was here when they cleaned to ask them to put additional chlorine in the pool...

...I could call one of my *tico* friends to see if he could fish it out of the water for me. I couldn't bring myself to touch it – it was just so scaly...and big...and dead.

Then I remembered there was one of those large nets that they use to clean the pool with near the wall. So I grabbed it, put it in the pool, and tried to scoop up the dead *garrobo*. But then the *garrobo* moved and swam into the middle of the pool (but still at the bottom). I again tried to scoop it up. And it moved to the other side. At this point, I'm happy that the *garrobo* is alive, but now its life is in my hands! If I can't get it into the net, it will surely drown. That's a lot of pressure to be under!

Several minutes go by of me trying to get the animal into the net, and it squirming around avoiding being captured.

At one point I yelled out, *"I'm trying to help you, get into the net!"*

To make matters worse, it had to have been 95 degrees that day and I was standing in full sun while trying to save this animal. Eventually I got it into the net, brought it out of the water and laid it on the ground. But it didn't move, it didn't leave the net. Oh _____ (fill in the blank again). Here I had tried to rescue it and it died anyways. So once again, I'm looking at this dead *garrobo* and wondering what I am going to do with it.

I take the pole, extend the net over the wall, and try to dump it out in the *zona verde*. After all, that's what I see the pool cleaners do with all of the leaf debris they collect each week. But for whatever reason, it was stuck in the net. So now

I'm trying to get the *garrobo* out of the net. After several attempts, it falls out of the net to the ground...and hooray!...I hear it scurry off into the underbrush. It must have just been playing opossum with me.

I don't know what the *garrobo* was thinking. I mean, I literally saw it dive from the wall into the pool. Perhaps he was trying to emulate Michael Phelps? Perhaps he wanted to cool off from the insanely hot day? I don't know...I'm just glad I managed to get it out of the pool before it drowned. I also hope he learned his lesson and I don't have to add lifeguard to the list of things I'm responsible for around here!

The step-by-step guide for removing a wolf spider from your home

One morning, I begrudgingly dragged myself out of bed at 5:30 a.m. after a fitful night of weird dreams, and got myself on the yoga mat for an intense 45 minute workout. Following that, I quickly downed my daily green juice (still dripping in sweat), and then proceeded to go into the bathroom and turn on the shower only to look down and see a wolf spider hanging out in the corner. A gigantic, furry, jumping, venomous wolf spider, slightly smaller than a tarantula.

Oh *dios mio*. Seriously? It was too early to be dealing with such mayhem in my home. Thankfully, I had that green juice to pump up my energy like Popeye and help me to deal with the situation.

So I started the task at hand by staring intently at it, but that seemed to bore the spider as it stretched out its front legs.

I left the light on in the bathroom (because they're nocturnal right?... so if there's a light on, it'll think it's daylight and go to sleep... right?) and started to pace around my house. Since I can get from one side to the other in about eight steps, that didn't get me very far. Meanwhile, all I could think about was how long this gigantic spider had been in my home and how he got in (and even more important, how am I going to get him out)?

I popped back into the bathroom and it was still stretched out in the corner. I took a photo of it and posted it on Facebook, leaving a comment for some local friends to see if they were nearby and not working yet (and maybe they could come and rescue this poor spider from my home). No reply... I was gonna have to deal with this one on my own.

I went into the kitchen and looked for my widest and tallest container. The only one that fit the description was a brand new one that I hadn't even used yet. I carefully nudged the spider out of the corner to get it under the container without cutting off any of its legs. Then I took a piece of paper and coaxed it under but it wasn't strong enough. So I found a piece of cardboard but that was too thick.

By this time, another local friend had commented that I should use a magazine cover. So while I don't normally buy magazines, I did recall having some old Nature Air magazines sitting on top of my fridge. I grabbed one and ripped off the cover. This, my friends, is why you should never throw anything away – you never know when you might need a magazine cover to deal with a spider.

That did it. As I nudged the cover underneath, the spider ran up the side of the tall container. Good. It was no longer hanging out along the bottom...less chance of an escape when I turn the canister over.

Okay. Now let's all just take a moment here and breathe.

I knew I didn't want to attempt to right the container until the spider had a chance to relax into its current position at the top of the canister. I chose this "relaxing" time to open my front door. After some time had passed, I very carefully lifted up the opposite sides of the paper and the container, placing it right side up on my shower floor. I quickly replaced the magazine cover with the container's lid and ran outside and downstairs to the open jungle lot next to my house. I then opened the lid and using a swinging motion with the container, released the spider, flinging him several feet out into the wild. Deep breath. It landed on a branch and went off on its merry way.

And people wonder what I do all day...

(Side note: that container is now what I use to hold my tea light candles. It does not contain food LOL)

Chapter 4

But It's Not Just About The Bugs & The Food:

The New Normal

"The ability to observe without evaluating is the highest form of intelligence."

Krishnamurti

Growing up and living in large suburbs in California, it was an adjustment learning how to go about daily life surrounded by small towns. While I was endlessly frustrated by the over-prevalent fast food and Starbucks offerings in the States, it was strange to find myself in places that less than 200 people called home. Before living in Costa Rica, when I'd pass through such towns I'd think, *"What do these people do here? There seems to be nothing there! No industry, very few restaurants, no stores, libraries... I can't even imagine living that way by choice."*

But over the years of living here, they've grown on me and I've come to understand there's a certain charm to these little towns.

When you consider that the entire country of Costa Rica has a population of about 4.7 million and I came from a State that had almost 40 million people, you get a good feel for my perspective.

I didn't miss sitting in traffic, the cars, the overwhelming numbers of people, the fast food restaurants on every corner... It is so calming to drive and walk around these little towns and just be able to breathe!

To see the simple life in action.

I also enjoy the predictability of each town – there is always a FÚTBOL field, a church, a bar, and a *soda* (a small family run restaurant). Not all towns have full-fledged schools but often a single classroom that teaches all grade levels. Everybody knows everybody, not unlike small towns in the States and yet still different. There was usually at least one *Super* (grocery store), sometimes more, but if not a *Super* then definitely a *pulperia*. If you were lucky you could also find a pharmacy or a hardware store but banks and ATM's were few and far between.

The small town that I live in now doesn't even have mail service. In places where there is, mail is delivered by motorcycle (can you imagine trying to deliver the mail by moto in the States?) and at the post office or at the grocery store, you can recharge a prepaid cell phone and pay utility bills.

I wish everyone could experience such a way of life for themselves, to fully understand just how different it is; that life really can thrive without the presence of a Starbucks on every corner.

My more isolated existence came with other benefits as well. I completely disconnected from trivia such as what the hottest celebrity wore to which award show, and which pop song was being routinely overplayed on the radio.

Even when snippets of info made it to me, I had no interest in tracking the full story down. There was some big to-do about Beyonce's hair? Meh. And the Kardashian's? I remain blissfully unaware of who they are. Admittedly, I didn't care so much about these things when living in California but it was definitely more prevalent and available there.

This wasn't the result of living in and around smaller towns though. It was also part and parcel of embracing the *tico* lifestyle - to only know about what I can see in front of me. I noticed the sun setting more to the south as I wrote outside on my terrace in November. If the clouds were rolling in from the Eastern mountains, we'd probably have rain in the afternoon.

It was incredibly peaceful to let go of so many details about the goings on of the world to focus on my own thoughts. What I see in front of me. This moment. That's where my focus is. I could breathe easier letting go of things that I no longer wanted or needed.

There were other aspects of the Costa Rica lifestyle that really impressed me. For example, imagine going into a Safeway or Whole Foods, picking up a few items, getting to the check-out line only to realize you only have $4 in your wallet and they don't take credit cards nor are there any ATMs in the vicinity. You'd probably find yourself picking out the most important items that add up to $4 and then having to let the rest go until you could go to the bank.

But in Costa Rica, it's a different story. For example, I ordered fresh cacao powder from Jorge at La Iguana Chocolate and he put it on the bus before I could even get to the bank to make the payment transfer.

One time at my local fruit and veggie market, I really did only have $4 in my wallet yet the owner rang up the items and put everything into my reusable bag for me. I kept showing him that I only had the 2,000 *colones* but he shook his head, smiled at me and told me, *"No worries, just bring the rest next time."*

It sounds straight out of a fictional small town in one of the Southern United States, but it's the reality in Costa Rica. It's one of the reasons I loved living in my new home. I found this trust and easy pace of life a nice reminder of the decency and kindness of others that is often lacking in more fast-paced societies.

Another piece of small town charm could be our lack of addresses...although that's open for debate. Even after several years of living here, my friends are still asking me if they can send me a package or a letter. I keep telling them,

"We don't have addresses here! Nor do we have mailboxes. Or street names."

The address of my first house literally could have been: *The House Behind the Guanacaste Tree*. Okay, that's a bit of an exaggeration but the truth is, instead of using street numbers and names, the address system uses points of reference (in the case of my first house, a nearby hotel), and then it's *xx* meters south and *xx* meters west of the hotel. Not all but many of the houses also have names, like Casa del Sol, or Casa Blanca.

Although sometimes that doesn't work.

When I first moved to Tamarindo, I went to the post office, told them the name of the house and they looked at me with bewildered stares. So I was asked to draw a map of where I lived, hoping the mail carrier would figure out how to find me, if and when I received mail. Now, I've given up. I don't get mail and I'm kind of okay with that.

Another example: I had to call DHL in order to give them my new address and redirect a delayed package that was going to my first house. When the woman asked me for my new address, I paused and said, *"Can I give you a tracking number for another package that has my new address?"* The woman agreed, and once she opened up that tracking number, she understood why and replied, *"Oh thank goodness you gave me the tracking number, I never would have understood the address if I hadn't seen it"*. It's just so bizarre and different from anything you'd ever see in the States!

My only real concern about not having an actual address is if all the points of reference will work if I ever have an emergency situation. Thankfully, that issue has not yet come up!

By far one of the best things about a small town is that people are always willing to help one another. One time, as I was driving home (in a rental car) from a few days away, I was about 15 minutes into the drive on the dirt road out of Guiones and came up to a small, one-lane bridge where the opposite direction had the right-of-way. There were several cars pulled over to the side and I quickly realized they were all parked, not crossing, because the river had overflowed onto the road on the other side. It had been raining extensively for the last few hours and as I often say about Costa Rica, a road can easily and quickly turn into a river.

Now... I've driven through a lot of rivers here...but I was never the one driving. A few minutes went by and a few cars drove through from the other side – all large SUV's. Still none of the cars on my side were attempting it.

One of the drivers from the other side parked his vehicle near mine and got out to talk with friends. I leaned out my window and asked them if I would be able to get through with the Rav4 and they said, *"Sure, no problem!"* But the Rav4 is a lot smaller than the Montero they were driving, which was not only bigger but had a higher clearance. One of them could sense the fear in me, walked over to the car and told me he'd drive my car across but I felt bad since he'd then have to walk through the muddy waters to the other side again.

So I shook my head and said I could do it. I waited for a larger SUV to go in front of me so I could follow them through. Being a dirt road and not being able to see the potholes (or where the river ended...or how deep the water actually was) made it that much more of an excruciating experience. There were times when the car felt like it was leaning to one side or the other, but I couldn't stop nor could I figure out how to get it to level out. It took a few minutes to get through and it was probably only 1 kilometer of driving. At the other side was a very long line of people, cars, and motorbikes, including a few police officers, waiting for the river to subside.

You would never know laundry could be so complicated

In my second house in Playa Langosta and in my current home, I have the strangest washing machine - it is borderline manual. To get the water into the machine, I have to turn on the water spigot at an outdoor sink which is attached to a hose, then I add soap and clothes. When I first used it, I always had to remember not to walk away at that point because otherwise, I thought it would be like an *I Love Lucy* episode with soap suds and water spilling out of the washer.

But actually no, I eventually learned that there is a safety valve that will drain the water before it overflows. Thank goodness! I do still have to remember to turn off the water though, which for me, who normally does eight things at once, is somewhat of a challenge. It's only happened once but that was after an hour of letting the water run as I accidently forgot I was doing manual laundry.

Not a good moment for this eco girl.

There was also one time when the hose leading into the washer was making all kinds of weird sounds. I went to fidget with it and, well, the hose flew off the top of the washer and since the water was on full force filling up the bin, it ended up going everywhere, including soaking me.

LOST AND FOUND IN THE LAND OF MAÑANA

Getting back to the actual washing part... After you turn off the water, you turn on the machine, and after 15 minutes, it just stops. From here, you twist one of the levers so that the water exits the machine and then you twist the lever again to close the drain - another step that I often forget because once the water is out of the machine, you then have to turn the water back on at the spigot to fill it up for the softener rinse. But often times, I forget to twist the little lever the second time and so the water continues to run out of the machine as I'm trying to put it in. Eventually though, I hear the water draining into the shower or the hole in the ground or just the ground itself (I've lived in a few houses with these archaic washers) and I remember to close the valve. So the water fills up again, I add softener, turn off the water, and select the number of minutes for the rinse cycle.

I then have to remember that the water needs to be drained again, and put the clothes in small batches into this little bucket attached to the washer which is about ¼ the size of the washer. This is the spin cycle. And because of its size, I have to spin multiple loads from the same wash. It's bizarre but seems to work. Kind of. If it's not balanced perfectly, the entire machine will shake and move.

One time, it spun all the way around and ended up against my screen door. Thankfully, that was the side door and I could get out the front door to move the machine back into place. My clothes seem, for the most part, clean and the spin cycle makes them less of a sopping wet mess. Then I untangle everything (one of the most irritating parts of this manual washer and which I swear is destroying my clothes) and grab my folding clothesline and hang everything to dry near the sunny window, which can often take up to two, sometimes three, days depending on the amount of humidity in the air.

Tico style innovation (and lack thereof)

When I lived in Tamarindo, I rented a car one day and drove to the "Do-It-Center" in Liberia. There I found a wooden clothes drying rack, which definitely proved to be useful on days when I need to dry my clothes but couldn't use an outdoor line.

When I moved to Manuel Antonio, my housekeeper saw the rack and was in total awe. She had never seen one before. She asked me where I got it and I told her she could probably find one in San Jose, although that's proven to be difficult now that the wooden one has broken. After it broke (surprise, surprise - everything breaks here), I tried to both super glue it together as well as hold it together with duct tape, but neither have worked well.

My property owner in Manuel Antonio hand washed a lot of her family's clothes. At first, I thought it was because the washing machine takes up too much energy (which I still think is part of the reason, as she's always stressed about the electricity bill). But what she told me is that the washer, a Kenmore, does not get her clothes as clean as she would like.

Well... I think there are a few different reasons for that. One: the washer did kinda suck. You actually had to start spinning the drum in order for the spin cycle to work. Two: she used the cheapest soap possible. Cheap is not better. Three: although the hot water heater for the building (this place did actually have lukewarm water) is next to the washer, it's not actually hooked up to the washer. And while washing clothes in cold water is better for the environment, it's also true that it doesn't get them as clean. The "Tide for Cold Water" product isn't just a marketing scheme.

Learning workarounds

When dealing with little things going wrong (and sometimes even big things going wrong) I've learned that sometimes, you just have to make adjustments to what you currently have.

Take for example the leaking freezer in my first house. Since it wasn't working and the contractor couldn't find the rubber thingie that goes around the edge to fix it, I was temporarily given the fridge/freezer from the owner's house (who lived in Italy). But the fridge had a three-prong, grounding plug and the owner and manager refused to install a proper outlet in the kitchen for me. I had asked previously because the electric kettle I purchased at a local Costa Rican store came with a three-prong plug and the only three-prong outlet in the house was in the living room. But instead of replacing the outlet when the fridge was brought over, the contractor just broke off the third piece of the plug. Simple as that. The fridge seems to work so I guess it's okay... (and it's not my fridge, after all).

Another interesting thing is how you pay contractors here. One contractor handed me his business card and on the back of the card was his bank account number and *cedula* (which is like a social security number). He asked me to transfer the money into his account, rather than paying by cash or credit card.

Of course, when I went to the bank, there were complications. First I was told that I had to have my real passport (not a paper copy) in order to transfer or withdraw money. My license and account number were not sufficient. So I went home and retrieved my passport from the safe. Upon my return, he then told me he must include a reason for the transfer of funds. WHY??? It's so very *big brother* here and I can't understand it. I thought I only had to explain *why* for dollar amounts over $1,000, but this was nowhere near that amount. I would come to learn that any time I made a deposit (cash or checks), or asked to make a transfer to a vendor or anyone for that matter, I would be asked what it was for.

I often wonder (in my head) what would happen if I responded with: *"Oh, I'm just doing a little money laundering."* Or, *"That was for the*

drug deal that went down last night. Gotta pay my dealer now."

But, I've just had to accept that nothing is easy here when it comes to the bank or the government. And to not ask why. A well-known but often unspoken mantra here is: **Make Easy Hard**. Picture lots of red tape.

Living in this "paradise", I experience many flashbacks to the 80's...

Remember when you used to get the huge catalogs from Best (I think that was the name of the department store) or Sears or JC Penny? And then you'd flip through them and pick out all the things you wanted (for me, being a kid, I always went straight for the toy section).

Well, I was doing just that recently when a friend's cousin brought me a catalog of furniture. I desperately needed a sofa in my first house and wasn't able to find one that was reasonably priced, and for which the delivery fee wasn't exorbitant. And just like the others, I paid her via her bank account and *cedula* number. I guess identity theft doesn't exist here because in the States, you'd never give out your social security number!

Another "80's Department Store" moment is when you go to the small chain stores that carry electronics and some kitchen items. Remember how you'd go to the large warehouse style stores in the 80's and you'd find something you want and then you'd let a sales associate know, you'd pay for it at the cashier and then go to another section of the store to get the item as it came off a conveyor belt?

Welcome to the 21st century in Costa Rica.

Let's say you want to buy a toaster. Seems simple enough, right? *Think again...* You can't just go and pick up the toaster, bring it to the cashier and buy it. Oh no. No no. You have to find someone to help you, they bring you to their computer, they take down your personal information (name, passport number/*cedula*, phone, etc), then you walk to the back of the store to pay a woman sitting at a desk (it's always a woman at the desk and a male sales associate – more on that later). But you have to give her your passport or cedula at that point as well. Even if you're paying cash.

Meanwhile, the original salesperson is locating the purchased item in the back of the store. Once you pay, you then find the original salesperson again and he walks you to the front of the store with the item, opens the item, takes it out to show you, packages it back up and you can now leave the store. There was even one time when I bought a fan and as I was leaving they stopped me, took my receipt and wrote down my name and purchase information in a book. *They hand wrote it in a book.* It was 2016.

Maybe you're thinking the reason they want your personal information is for returns. Except here's the thing: In Costa Rica, there are no returns. How I miss Costco and Nordstrom and their awesome return policies.

LOST AND FOUND IN THE LAND OF MAÑANA

The only way to return an item here is if it breaks and even then, they won't give you a new one. They'll take it and send it to a repair shop. I've known people who have had to return refrigerators and had to wait for weeks for the repair. All the while, they had no refrigerator.

To Ticos, all of this is normal. They know no other way of doing things. To me, it's a little upside down bizarro.

And then there's "tico time" ... now some might find "*Tico time*" charming. Me - that's still a debate. 30 minutes is never 30 minutes here – it's more like an hour. *"I'll see you at 4:00"* really means 5:00. Or 5:30. Or maybe not at all. It takes some getting used to and it's definitely difficult to make plans because I find myself always waiting around.

One day, I had hired a taxi to pick me up at 11:00, knowing I had multiple errands outside of town, and I needed to be back by 2 in order to meet with DHL. But 11:00 came and went. So as I waited for the taxi watching the minutes pass by, I could honestly feel my body start to stress. I kept telling myself, "*I know, I know, this is 'Tico time'*". But, honestly, I don't understand it.

Everyone I meet seems to own a watch so I don't understand how no one is ever on time! I never wear a watch but somehow I know what time it is and where I'm supposed to be at any given moment.

It's amazing to me that anything ever gets done here and it's no wonder everything takes longer than it should. Everything is always about *mañana* (tomorrow) because they really do lose track of time.

Still today, several years later, I'm trying to get used to this different way of life but I always feel like I'm on a delay and that never makes me feel good. I have many things to do and I can't be waiting around for people who may or may not show up!

So on that particular day, the taxi did show up eventually and then DHL came early. I was still out running errands (although I would have been home had the taxi shown up on time) but the DHL guy was kind enough to call me and then wait for me, even though that probably set him back a little time in his schedule as well. I guess their relaxed schedules sometimes work in my favor. But when I told him I'd be there in 15 minutes, I was there in 15 minutes! Only because I had cut short my errand running in order to get back to meet with him.

And perhaps I should realize that these couple things aren't a big deal, but it's not just a couple...

Buses – they stop whenever someone wants to get on or off. There was one girl who had the bus driver stop outside of a bank and the driver waited for her while she stood in line at the ATM. This is a great example of why nothing gets done and everyone is always late. Yes, it was very kind of the driver but, from where the bus picked her up, she could have easily walked to the ATM and waited for the next bus to come around.

Work doesn't always get done when you think it should. Like, I had a leak under my kitchen sink that was flooding my kitchen, dining room, and living room (in a 400 square foot apartment), and it took ten days to fix. There was so much water that I was literally walking in puddles and had to go into my storage bins to find more towels (since I didn't have a dryer).

Nothing is ever done on schedule. They may tell you that it will be done by March. What you learn is that really means May or possibly even November. Or the March of the following year.

It's a chaotic environment, nothing works the way it should. Water is even on its own time schedule and only comes out of the faucet or showerhead when it wants. The electricity flickers on and off, often on a nearly daily basis.

Everything breaks here. Part of it is just my living in a small space and not having enough room for everything.

The other part is - I truly believe this - that Costa Rica gets all the second-hand products from China that wouldn't pass quality control in the United States. China did build the new stadium in San Jose so there is just cause for my belief.

There are actually knock-offs like the famous Simpson's "Sorny" (instead of Sony). One example is Py-ro-ex. It's not Pyrex. Trust me, generic is not "just as good". What it is, in reality, is a waste of money as you'll end up spending twice as much to either replace the item in a year or have it fixed.

In my apartment in Manuel Antonio, there was a huge flat screen Panasonic TV – probably 50 inches - but the color was all messed up and the owner told me that even though it was only a few years old, they already had it repaired once. When they took it back to the repair place, it was gone for three months. When they brought it back, it worked...for a short time. Within a month, the color was strange again, and within two months, the television set was totally dead. But then the property owners had no place to put it, so they left it up on the wall and brought me another smaller television which sat on a small table below the big screen.

I've also had things break here that then start working again.

The a/c adapter for my laptop, for example. And the vacuum cleaner (another miracle product that my housekeeper loves and hadn't ever seen in the past). My printer once told me for weeks that there was paper jammed inside of it (there wasn't) and then about a month later, it just started working again. Although the printer's wifi has never worked.

I've gone through five blenders in three years. The last one - every time I used it, I thought it was going to catch fire as it started to smell as if the motor was burning. I finally broke down and bought a Ninja which cost me nearly 3 times what I would have paid in the States. And even then, one of the smoothie cups broke and I had to get a replacement from friends visiting from the US! My Oral-B electric toothbrush has died numerous times only to come back to life (and no, it wasn't just an issue of being left off the charger for too long!)

But that's also why you always keep everything…just in case. Mind you, it may be sounding like I'm a bit of a hoarder but trust me, I'm not! It's just so difficult to find things here that it's important to store random stuff for that random moment when you may need it.

For example, I recently broke the glass portion of my Bodum coffee press. My housekeeper had broken the "plunger press" part of the first one I had bought, but I had kept the glass jar. So, I now have a complete set again. *Voilà.* So simple. I never let my housekeeper clean the Bodum again!

My morning coffee ritual is *muy importante.*

I've had a set of Calvin Klein sheets since 1998. So *so* soft - I love them. And since living here, they've ripped twice and both times I've had a seamstress sew them back together. The second time I actually tried to superglue the ripped section but that didn't work so well.

Another example, a friend once asked me if I had any spare fan blades as one of his blades had broken. (I didn't)

A lot of what's in my house is held together by super glue and duct tape. These two items are absolutely essential for living in Costa Rica. Consider it a part of one's "living in the tropics emergency kit".

Chapter 5

Every rose has its thorn

"Alice: But I don't want to go among mad people.

The Cat: Oh, you can't help that. We're all mad here. I'm mad. You're mad.

Alice: How do you know I'm mad?

The Cat: You must be. Or you wouldn't have come here."

Lewis Carroll

LOST AND FOUND IN THE LAND OF MAÑANA

While Costa Rica undeniably has some old-fashioned charm to its pace of life, along with that comes a less modern system for doing just about everything.

In some ways, Costa Rica is similar to the Wild West of the 1800s (minus the more dramatic O.K. Corral-type duels).

Besides the literal similarities: dirt roads, cowboys riding their horses alongside the highways, and prostitution being legal, there is also a cavalier attitude towards things like wearing seatbelts and drinking alcohol in public, which are overlooked by the police.

Stop signs and stop lights are merely "suggestions". Women look for husbands to settle down, while married men are at the "saloon".

At the 100 day mark, my bubble of living in paradise burst. Life here became forever tainted.

On my 99th night in the country I endured my first burglary. Someone broke in through my kitchen's sliding glass door while I was sleeping upstairs and stole everything they could get their hands on. Thankfully, they did not see my laptop (the life blood of my business and only source of income), which was hidden underneath the microwave cart. They did, randomly, steal my pitcher full of *tamarindo* juice from the fridge. And also the 1974 silver dollar coins that my dad had bought for me the year I was born. They probably weren't worth much... except of course, in sentimental value.

Thankfully neither Harmony or I were hurt.

Everyone I knew told me that they had been robbed as well... at least once. And everyone told me it was my housekeeper *("it's always the housekeeper"),* or probably her husband. I didn't want to believe them as I really liked her. I had her coming to my house twice a week and was paying her an above-average rate. But a few days after the burglary, she arrived at my house with my wallet which contained my license, passport and debit cards. (They just wanted the cash - $200.) She told me she found the items in the dirt outside my house but I had gone out several times and never seen them. I was grateful to not have to go to the Embassy in San Jose for a new passport but it was just too much of a coincidence.

A friend told me that she would go with me to the drug dealers' houses in Tamarindo to see if they had my stolen items and to find out if they'd let me buy the stolen items back (besides the coins and cash, my camera, iPod, all my chargers, as well as many other belongings had been taken, totaling about $2,000).

No, I am not making this up.

What I've come to see as somewhat amusing is that the *Ticos* will always insist that it's not a *Tico* who has committed the crime. It's always someone from Nicaragua or some other poorer Latin American country. Like the maid, my *Tico* friends said, *"She must be from Nicaragua".* (No, actually she was *Tica*).

After the robbery, I did file a police report. (Oh, I was so naïve thinking anything would come of that!) The police officer followed me home, however

I really didn't understand why. He didn't take any fingerprints or note anything other than what I had already told him at the station.

Then as he was going to leave, he literally leaned in and tried to kiss me...on the mouth. Oh, and did I forget to mention that he had told me that he was married and had children?

Seriously, one cannot make this up.

After that, because he knew where I lived and had my number from the police report, he started calling me at all hours of the night and even showed up in my backyard at one point. That was the final straw.

Harmony and I moved out two weeks later. While I moved to a much more secure building, I have never been able to shake the feeling of fear that came over me from that experience. It's a sad coincidence that my second book is called *No Fear* and now I live in fear every day.

I was bummed when I moved. I loved that house. It was the house the universe had given me after my direct request to live somewhere just as beautiful as Jicaro. The private pool with the big backyard that backed onto a green zone, filled with monkeys and iguanas and colorful birds - it was my Costa Rican dream come true. But it wasn't safe. And there were a lot of scorpions. And of course, the cop who was stalking me.

My experiences with gringos...

My circle of close friends and even wider circle of acquaintances in the States had a distinct absence of abusive partners, alcoholics, drug users, thieves, cheaters, liars and prostitutes, however, upon settling in Costa Rica I soon crossed paths with all of the above.

Of course, my Stateside friends and I weren't perfect but we aspired to live calm, conscious and peaceful lives.

Here, it wasn't just that people engaged in these things on the rare occasion but rather as their daily M.O. It was completely new to me and more than a little disconcerting.

On relationships...

The relationship codes of conduct here have been difficult to reconcile with my personal belief in monogamy, commitment and trust. Amongst the gringos, there's always gossip about so-and-so's husband sleeping with so-and-so. All of this was occurring under the microscope of a small town culture where everyone knew everyone else's business. Of course, the States has its share of unfaithful people, but I'd yet to experience the phenomenon as prevalently (and publicly) as some of the people around me seemed wont to do. I'm sure, given my tone in this paragraph, that it goes without saying that I don't believe cheating to be acceptable behavior in a relationship, so the various couples that stayed together despite the gossip surrounding their marriage was hard for me to understand.

Tamarindo certainly earned the nickname, "Dramarindo" because of the ongoing mini-scandals and the buzz that would accompany them. It's also called "Land of the Misfit Toys", but what I've personally named it is "Neverland". People there don't grow up - they're Peter Pans. And sadly, that's my experience of most of the expat beach communities in Costa Rica.

Another popular nickname is "Tamagringo"... because there are only a handful of *Ticos* who can actually afford to live in the town. And I truly do mean a handful. The majority of *Ticos* live just outside of town in Villa Real or Huacas and come into town to work or go to the discotheques at night (which, by the way, are open until the sun rises).

I've come to learn from the locals that Tamarindo was an unknown, uninhabited area up until about 15-20 years ago. But, as it was on a beach, foreigners started going there to surf and saw an opportunity to develop a community. They built homes and businesses and now it truly is a 21st century version of the Wild West.

When I lived there, only the main road was paved and that's all of a few miles long at most. The rest of the roads were dirt. There's a tiny police station but people don't follow any laws since they know the police won't do anything (or they'll start stalking you). I was often told never to stay out past midnight because that's when the scene gets really bad. You know... like, people get murdered...

Living The High Life, Or Not

There is a party/drug culture here that both *Ticos* and *gringos* participate in (*gringos* being from basically anywhere other than Central America – even my Argentinean friends are called *gringos* by some *Ticos*). In comparison to the *Ticos* however, the *gringos* usually have quite a bit more money, which affords them the opportunity to party harder and with more expensive drugs and alcohol. Plus they rarely have a set schedule, with no real job waiting for them in the morning, so there's time to be hungover and kick back at the beach with a *hair of the dog* drink.

In case you weren't aware (and it seems many people here in Costa Rica aren't), drugs are not good for you... at all. It would be totally irresponsible of me to take drugs – for my own body, mind, heart and spirit. I want to treat my body with lovingkindness, and therefore, I'm not going to put poison into it. (Plus, using drugs is not my definition of fun.) To truly be a source of joy and lovingkindness, and to create the life that I want, I need to find it within...without the aid of external stimulus.

> I can't show up and do good things if I'm constantly in an alternate reality or recovering from a hangover.

LOST AND FOUND IN THE LAND OF MAÑANA

I've always had a strong sense of self. Not sure if it was my parents' doing, the *Just Say No* campaign, the 8th grade DARE program, or just the simple fact that I always wanted to be in control, but I never used drugs while living in California. Ever. Not as a teen. Not even when I went down to Tijuana at the age of 16 (and came back with what was probably the worst hangover of my life). Sure I smoked cigarettes and drank like a fish sometimes, but no drugs ever entered my body. And not to lessen the damaging effects of smoking and drinking but at least those are legal in all 50 States.

Now, unfortunately, I can no longer say that I've never used drugs. When my sweet Harmony passed away in March 2013, my friends in Tamarindo thought the best way to support me was to get me high.

I didn't know the cookie they told me to eat had pot inside it. This was not a Bill Clinton situation of *"I didn't inhale"*. This was truly an Alice in Wonderland situation of *"eat this"*. I had just buried my 18-year-old cat - who I had adopted when he was three weeks old - between the roots of an old *pochote* tree surrounded by red hibiscus flowers and hummingbirds, and I didn't even think that I should perhaps ask what's inside the cookie.

(Sadly, I now know to always ask.)

I'm grateful for the people who helped me out on this terribly sad day and this, I suppose, was how they would handle the situation in their own life. However, while it did make me more numb to the pain (combined with the many mojitos that followed), I still woke up the next morning, dealing with the loss; knowing that Harmony was gone. Likely, many of them would have grabbed their bong or pipe and taken a hit so that they could remain in this unfeeling state. Day in and day out.

I don't want to live unconsciously. I want to experience life. The good and the bad. Even when it hurts.

As a teenager, pretty much all of my friends used drugs and some pretty hard core ones at that. But no one in my peer group ever tried to force me into using whatever they were taking. They all understood that I wasn't into that and they respected my beliefs. And they would never, *ever*, deceive me into using them. Even the guy I was dating (who grew pot in his closet) would have kicked anyone's ass who tried to pressure me into using drugs.

I thought I had put behind me the days of standing on cliffs with tripped out friends, trying to explain to them that there were no stairs leading down to the beach.

Until I moved to Costa Rica.

I was once again faced with all the same types of people that I hung out with in high school. Only we weren't 16 anymore. (We weren't even 25.) These people are 30+, some even have children, and they are still getting stoned, drunk, high, and blitzed out of their minds on x, acid and coke - sadly, on a somewhat regular basis.

LOST AND FOUND IN THE LAND OF MAÑANA

I was once again having people do lines of coke in front of me. It was no longer with the $100 bills that my high school friends' parents gave them on a Friday night, but it was still a line of white powder being snorted up their nose more than 20-30 years after the age I (so wrongly) believed most people stopped doing this activity.

And while I always felt accepted by my group of friends in high school, that isn't how I feel here. Or it could be that I just don't want to involve myself with these people, so I'm not really trying to be well-liked or to fit in. I don't need to be a part of the popular clique if the popular clique means getting drunk and high.

One friend actually told me that if you don't party, you won't have any friends or anything to do here. Sadly, she's correct. Thankfully, I don't care. I don't want to spend my energy caring for people who think there are stairs on the steep rocky cliff. As a teenager, no problem. But now, at 40+ years of age, no thank you.

For the most part, I have very little in common with the people who use hard core drugs. The pot smokers don't bother me as much, other than the fact that I don't see them doing very much with their lives and that saddens me. It's incredibly boring. I knew a lot of pot smokers in Sonoma County but at least those people were doing something, they had meaning in their lives beyond themselves.

Even the people who you may think are all into health and wellness, they too are using drugs. I've known people to take hash, on a somewhat regular basis, and be blitzed out of their minds for days at a time while they're trying to run a wellness business. And trust me, it does not make you a smarter, more efficient person. Based on my experiences with them, it was quite the opposite.

I believe part of the problem is that these people just don't have goals. Sure, they may own businesses and have families, but they don't see any bigger picture outside of themselves and their group of friends. Again, very much a teenager's reality. When one of them dies (and several actually have since I've lived here), everyone is so shocked. Of course, it's a horrible tragedy, but honestly, it's not shocking whatsoever. If you continuously engage in risky behavior, there are often times negative consequences.

Sadly, I've known more people here in Costa Rica, in just the first 4 years of living here, to die from an overdose, be murdered or commit suicide than I know in the first 37 years of my life, living in California.

So the standard, mainstream, foreigner culture here is drugs, alcohol, parties, lies and cheating. They don't do much during the day. They either own a business and often times illegally hire foreigners rather than supporting the local *Ticos*, or they have an illegal job, working under the table, but that's just so they can party more the next night. It's a very transient and day-by-day culture.

Again why I call this the land of *mañana*.

Trying to find compassion for the functioning drug addicts

Since I have yet to find that happy medium, as a part of my yoga practice I know I must practice lovingkindness - ahimsa.

Addiction (whether it's drugs, alcohol, abuse, lying, cheating, sex, food) is a mental illness, so how can I find compassion for them? My first reaction is to ask why I'm surrounded by this? But then I think, "Why do people choose this? What are the challenges in addiction and recovery? What is the drug culture and lifestyle?"

Since I'm surrounded by this culture every day, how do these things really affect one's life (since it's not my choice and I can't fully understand).

And what is its ripple effect on others?

One of my favorite books (and one of the few that I brought with me when I moved) is Lama Surya Das' *Awakening the Buddha Within.* Its pages are well-weathered and well-read. He writes that, while he may have experimented with drugs in the past, mostly to enhance his spirituality practice (not necessarily to just "party"), he now finds so much more pleasure in living a mindful life without them.

It's teachers and people like this who I seek to connect with here, and yet find it so difficult to actually do so. I don't want my path to be one of isolation, but at the moment, it seems to be my only healthy, balanced, mindful choice.

Also, one of the main reasons I felt lost for those first few years.

Another thing I truly can't understand are the drug-using expats who have children. These adults seemed to have carried the party lifestyle of their 16-year-old selves into their adult lives. Don't they want their kids to grow up to be mature and responsible adults? It seems like they are setting the bar for their offspring really, really low. Yes, many of them are trust fund kids so no matter what, their children will be taken care of and well educated so maybe they don't need to be good role models and can indeed live their party lifestyle without any repercussions (that we can see in this moment).

My belief is: If you don't grow up, and stop using drugs and partying when you have kids, that's a conscious choice. Might I say again...drugs are not good for you. They can kill you. Is that the legacy you want to leave for your children? That you led some rock star life (without the actual fame and celebrity) and now your kids are without parents because you couldn't (or wouldn't) grow up?

See, I still get mad. I'm still working on being mindful and compassionate. It's a daily practice.

In talking with a friend in the States about the expat communities here, she said she wasn't surprised to learn there were a lot of drugs and parties. She felt that most of these people couldn't make it in the real world (aka the US), and have thus found a place where they are accepted, with others who are also on the fringe of society.

But then she asked me the pivotal question... *"But that's not why you moved there, right? You didn't move to escape or run away from something?"*

No, I ran *to* something. I ran to a healthier, better, and what I hoped would be a more productive and meaningful life. I wanted to live fully and experience life, not totally understanding that I would be living in the land of *mañana*, and the challenges that would come with that. I didn't know the people here would make that much more difficult, testing my every notion of what living an intentional, mindful life means.

It's interesting, because I always thought I was a bit of a rebel when I was in the States, not one to follow the status quo of society. But here, it's taken to another level and I just can't drink the Kool-Aid.

It's like they're on a perpetual holiday where the party never ends.

For me this quote is so very appropriate:

I would rather die a meaningful death than to live a meaningless life. - *Corazon Aquino*

Unlike many of these "wanderlusters" who I've met along the way, I didn't come here with only a backpack and the thought that it would be cool to travel around the country a bit, work a few illegal jobs here and there, and just get by. To live the "laptop lifestyle" that's so popular these days. Trust me, I didn't even know what lifestyle design was when I moved here!

I also didn't come here to hide in an expat community and not fully embrace and respect living in someone else's country.

The vacationers and expats who come here and expect the cities and restaurants to celebrate 4th of July with fireworks and Thanksgiving with turkey, make me nauseous.

Sadly, the cities and restaurants cater to the vacationers and expats as they have the most money and we do actually celebrate both of those holidays, neither of which are a custom of Tico culture.

No wonder there's so much racism and dislike towards gringos by Ticos! *(more on that to come...)*

Ticos May Be The Happiest People In The World But...

I honestly cannot understand the drug culture here. Ticos or gringos. How can you be truly happy if a. you're living in survival mode and b. you're always on drugs and never truly experience REAL LIFE!

For many of the ticos who I've met, they're usually more into just smoking pot over the harder drugs. Although I know in certain areas of the country, there is some usage of cocaine and hallucinogenics – San Jose, Nosara, Tamarindo, Coco, Manuel Antonio to name a few. Just like in the States, you'll find it in beach communities and big cities alike - generally, where there's more money and more tourism.

But the pot smoking, it's every single day. Tico friends try to tell me that it's the same as my choosing to drink wine or beer. Except here's the difference: I don't drink alcohol when I first wake up and I don't need it (or want it) every day!

I'm not sure if it's a cultural conditioning that keeps Ticos acting like teenagers well into adulthood. Even their rites of passage are different. Many who live in the beach communities or other rural areas don't get driver's licenses when they turn the legal age (why would they – most don't even have cars when they're adults).

Many don't have bank accounts, even when they become adults. Nor do many have real jobs with real paychecks from which they have to pay taxes. Even though education is free, many never go to university or even graduate from high school. Many have babies when they're just young teens.

And of course, all of the above can be found in the US, but it just seems like I know and see so many more people here with these traits than I ever knew there.

This is what is just so different for me, coming from the States where so many people are trying their hardest to succeed and prosper, I don't understand how Ticos can be so content with their simple lives. Don't they get bored? Don't they want to have meaning in their life beyond rice and beans, surf and *fútbol*?

Note: I want to clarify again that not all ticos are like this. But I seem to attract the majority of these types into my life. It could just be where I'm living... perhaps the city is different...Although in speaking with others, I've been told that's not the case. The city is just as bad.

Some also seem to lack knowledge of societal living. I often wonder if they just don't learn manners here? I'm all for not following many of society's "rules" but there are some that I believe are just good manners.

Like... I knew one man who opened a Nutella jar in the supermarket, tore off the safety foil, stuck his finger in the jar, tasted it, didn't like it, put the lid back on and put it back on the shelf. I was horrified, to say the least. He was not 5 years old. He was 35. He was university educated and came from a good family.

There's also a well-known (but not often talked about) issue of Ticos leaving trash behind, anywhere and everywhere. Littering is not looked down upon and just accepted as status quo. Cutting in line is another one.

Saying no is not allowed here. They believe it's less offensive to just not show up, or show up hours late, then to call ahead and cancel, or text and say they're running late. Avoidance is a huge issue. Especially when it comes to communication.

There's also a lack of sensitivity.

Countless times I've had some rather hurtful things said to me, by different people, like: *"Why are you so fat?"* And, *"You're so old and you don't have any kids? What's wrong with you?"*

To them, these comments aren't disrespectful, offensive or rude.

With their strong ties to Catholicism, it's difficult for me to understand how *Ticos* justify their actions. Especially the big stuff like lying and cheating and stealing and even getting pregnant as a teenager (no sex before marriage, right?), but also the little things like being inconsiderate and insensitive. To me, it's all incongruent with their strong sense of religion. They go to church but they don't follow through with the promises they make to their God. Do we need to revisit the Ten Commandments? Trust me, many of those commandments are broken here on a daily basis and it's totally accepted.

Is this their definition of happiness? To lie, steal, cheat, use drugs, get drunk, have no responsibilities, never show up on time, and never really grow up? They can run back to mom's house if they get fired from a job and she'll cook for them and do their laundry, and even pay their cell phone bill.

In Spanish, *ganar* is translated as *to win*, not *to earn*. It's like they feel as if they deserve to have a paycheck, even if they do a crappy, careless job. I've actually had several people, *ticos* and *gringos* (one *tico* who was even in a fairly well-respected government role), tell me that *ticos* feel that they are "entitled". That seems to be the buzzword as it's what all of them have said. They are entitled to their way of *pura vida* lifestyle, where personal responsibility and common sense are so totally lacking.

Sometimes I wonder if they have any idea of what earning money really means. If you fire someone here, there is no unemployment insurance. It is you, the business owner, who has to pay them to leave (on top of their regular salary), even though they weren't doing their job *and* they're being fired! So there's really no incentive for anyone to do a good job because they get paid either way.

And even then, there are complications, and they can go to the government offices and get them to force a business owner to let them keep their job, even if they're *not doing* their job! There's also the mandatory annual bonus, one month's salary, every year at Christmas - the *alguinaldo* - that every working *Tico* is entitled to, even if they were fired from their job earlier in the year. They're rewarded for doing bad work. It's just so crazy to me!

I was told one story about a man who was working for a company and despite being totally incompetent and not having any idea what he was doing, his boss considered him *buena gente* (good people), and that had he been bilingual, he would have been able to keep the job.

So what that tells me is that it has nothing to do with competence. If you're a nice person, you can continue to work here in Costa Rica even if you don't know what you're doing. Of course, I also think that this man was only working 10 hours a week - at most - and totally ripping off the company as he was being paid a full time wage. But that seems to be okay. Because, again, he was *buena gente*.

It's no wonder there is so little growth and innovation here.

I knew another person who had 9 jobs in under 4 years. These were professional, white-collar type jobs. Imagine what that Curriculum Vitae looks like! Very few professional businesses in the US would hire someone with that kind of background.

Okay, so part of this tirade might have to do with my being a Generation X, and my issue with millennials thinking they deserve rewards without work. Or the way my parents raised me to be independent and self-sufficient. I definitely could not go running home to mom and dad if I was fired.

Lastly, as I briefly mentioned, there is the racism.

I can't understand how you can be so truly happy if you're also so very racist.

If it was just towards the gringos who have come in and taken over the country, I could try to have some understanding.

Although I do prefer a mosaic of culture compared to a monoculture.

But I've talked with so many *Ticos* who are racist against people from Nicaragua as well as racist against other *Ticos*!

It seems that, *again from what I've been told by Ticos*, the lighter your skin is, the wealthier and more opportunities you have in this country. If you have darker skin, you are usually less educated, poorer and opportunities for growth and change are rare.

Sadly, I've found this to be often the case. Most of the *Ticos* I know who are more "white-looking" went to good schools, some even in the US and often come from wealthy families. My *Tico* friends with darker skin are more often the ones in less professional jobs and have had less opportunities.

Finding the light in the dark side of paradise

Mind you, I don't want to live in a bubble. I chose to move here. I want to experience life here. All of it. The good and the not-so-ideal.

Living here, I've come to learn... it's not all pretty. But really, is any place truly perfect?

Someone once told me that the beach where I live in Manuel Antonio was "ghetto". It was definitely not the paradise she had anticipated.

At first, I was confused since Manuel Antonio is often listed as one of the top ten beaches in the world. What I came to realize was that she was referring to the actual town of Quepos, with its razor wire sitting atop high walls, creating compounds for rundown houses with tin roofs and tin siding.

While that was my first impression during my vacation in 2009, as I've come to learn and appreciate, that's Central America. And that's where I want to be.

If I wanted to live in the suburbs like Tamarindo attempts to be, I'd continue living in the States with easy access to Target, Costco, Whole Foods and Trader Joe's.

While trudging through some of the muddy water here hasn't been all that pretty, I have learned to be grateful for all the little things.

What brought me here in the first place...and what keeps me here.

Chapter 6

Does "Pura Vida" mean what you think it means?

"In order for the light to shine so brightly, the darkness must be present."

Francis Bacon

I would love to say that the mantra of Costa Rica, "*pura vida*", is similar to that of "*namaste*" in India and the yoga/buddhism world. Other than saying it as a greeting or a response to "thank you", these ideas are worlds apart. *Namaste*, in its simplest terms, means: "the Light in me honors and respects the Light in you."

I know I'm not going to be well-liked for this, criticizing the mantra of an entire country, but... there is no deep meaning to *pura vida*. I've actually polled random people and they all tell me it just means: "You're welcome", "Hello", "I'm good". I don't know why they honor a phrase that's just slang for "hello". (We have a word for that in English too – it's "hi".)

I once had someone I know well tell me (during a somewhat heated argument) that I'd never understand the concept of *pura vida*.

He may be right. I understand the concept of *namaste*. But *pura vida*, to me, is just a greeting and a way to not deal with life when it goes awry. Especially since I've started to see the use of *pura vida* as an excuse to not deal with, well, anything.

Your car breaks down? Your boyfriend cheats on you? Your house gets burgled? Your girlfriend is screaming at you for cheating on her? It's all *pura vida*... don't worry, *pura vida*.

My main issue when friends of mine use it as a response to, "How are you?" is that it seems like you're not allowed to answer with anything but "good" or "*pura vida*". Not deeply connecting with others in a real way. Everything is always "a-ok".

One time, when I answered the question "How are you" with honesty - that life was kind of a mess – my friend simply couldn't handle it. He contacted one of our mutual friends (a more mature, kind friend) to deal with me as it just wasn't acceptable for me to respond in such a negative way. He actually didn't respond to me at all after that text.

> Life is real, people. I don't often swear but truly, shit happens. Sometimes, reality bites. I should be allowed to experience how I feel in that moment and not have to soften it for another person's comfort. Especially not to someone who I considered a good friend.

I knew a woman in California many years ago who told me she was taking Paxil, an anti-depressant. But she chose to stop because it made her feel numb. Her way of describing it...her words... *my house could have been on fire and I would have just continued to go about my day, not caring.*

House burns down...Okay, well here, that would just be *pura vida*.

I don't understand this mentality. I honestly don't know if I ever will.

My friend's story is what I think about in terms of the way Pura Vida is used here.

Yes, being devoid of all feelings might be one way to live life. Or, it could be just another excuse to remain numb and do nothing with one's life - to not accept what is happening, to allow the house to burn down without having a single care, to completely avoid reality, and live in some fantasyland.

As much as I love Alice in Wonderland, I'm really starting to dislike Fantasyland.

Ignoring reality will only get you so far. The problems you're facing usually don't "go away" on their own - we have to learn how to manage daily life, and not pretend that everything is *"pura vida"* all the time.

I also believe *pura vida* prevents people from having real, honest, beautiful relationships.

I was once told that it was totally okay to lie to your spouse about your whereabouts, even if there was nothing questionable going on.

The saying: *"Ask for forgiveness, not for permission" is* pervasive and rampant here.

I've experienced it firsthand, in both my personal and professional relationships. It's all about the moment and what that person wants in that moment. My ex went on to tell me that everyone lies in order to avoid the jealous fights that would inevitably occur.

So they live in this la-la land where no one is honest or authentic with each other, and they all just maintain the *pura vida* / everything is okay vibe.

While some people will tell you that *pura vida* has its roots in "being in the present moment", it's nothing like mindfulness.

> Mindfulness acknowledges that things are happening.
> *Pura vida* chooses to ignore whatever is happening.

Mindfulness allows for pain to be experienced, acknowledging that suffering is optional. The reverse can be said for *pura vida,* pain is avoided but suffering is always underlying the numb state of being.

There are a few people here who can use the term *pura vida* without making me cringe when I hear it.

But the difference is, they're not living their life in an ignorant, avoidant state. They're showing up, they work hard (really hard), and they task themselves with continuous growth in both their personal and professional lives. And they allow me to have a bad day. They allow themselves to have a bad day. That is the *pura vida* that I can believe. The acceptance of the good and the bad and always trying to do more to better oneself.

Like *pura vida*, *"Tuanis"* is a loaded word for me. *Tuanis* means that you're a cool person, easy going, nice. I've been called *tuanis* by some *tico* friends. But as soon as I'm having a bad day, I'm no longer *tuanis* and they don't want to talk with me.

Here's the thing...

You *must* feel sadness in order to feel joy.

There's a yin and yang to everything. In order for there to be sunshine, there must also be a moon and darkness. In order for there to be a rainbow, we must have both sunshine and rain. We have to experience both pain and beauty, and to fully live in the world, we must know and understand both sides. How do you know what real happiness is if you've never been sad?

I once overheard a conversation between a Tico friend and his gringa girlfriend where the girlfriend kept repeating that she was sad. My friend kept repeating, *"I don't understand"* and he honestly couldn't.

I could hear the frustration grow in her voice as she said, *"Why can't you just be sympathetic towards me?"* This girl was new to town and very new to the *tico* culture, so while it was disheartening, I was also somewhat intrigued, listening to the two of them go round and round about his lack of feelings and compassion towards her. At one point, he actually got a bit angry and frustrated as well. The whole situation was sad but typical.

Maybe they don't feel they have permission to feel sad, after all, they're supposed to be living in the happiest country in the world.

I've given myself permission, and we all have permission, to feel all the different feelings there are...and then let them go. I may be angry, frustrated and disappointed with my client who doesn't pay, my team member who takes off on a surf trip without meeting her deadline (or even telling me she's going), or my housekeeper who doesn't show up. But then I have to let it go. I can choose to terminate my commitments with each of them (knowing that I'll probably just face the same problems with someone else), or I can choose to put up with it. Or I can find another way to handle it.

There is always a way, options, alternatives, choices. That is being innovative and growing! It took me some time to get to that place of understanding, but I did finally and it's a much more easeful place to live.

First I give myself permission to acknowledge the pain and then challenge myself to find the best solution possible in that moment. I also have to understand that they may not realize that in my culture, their actions are indeed offensive. Here, it's totally normal to not show up, to not call, to not pay, to not do the work.

And it's all ¡*pura vida!*

That's why the joke is that it will be done *mañana. Mañana* does not mean tomorrow here. It means *someday... maybe.*

They definitely have a different way of living here, and perhaps my acquaintance is right, I never will understand the real meaning of *pura vida.*

Beyond the laziness that I feel is prevalent within this culture, I do try to see it from the point of view that they've accepted this is their life. They may have a home that has a dirt floor, have a fifth grade education, and get pregnant when they're 14, but they've accepted that all that is okay. They don't need more. This is their life and this is what is normal for them.

I realize this may sound overly capitalist (which is so not me), but I feel like I would want to ask them this question...*don't you want more?* Don't you want to do more with your life, to improve your living conditions, to grow and learn and open your mind to all the different experiences life has to offer?

I'm not saying that they need a complete Apple Suite of products, but just simply what I'd consider basics – like a tile floor instead of dirt, a washing machine instead of doing everything by hand, and for my wanderlust self...the ability to travel. Even just to travel around and explore their own country.

I understand living simply (trust me, for the majority of my years here, I've lived in 400 square feet), but the way some of them live seems to be taking simplicity to the extreme considering we're now in the second decade of the 21st century.

Why isn't there a curiosity and the desire to explore, to know more than what they see in front of them?

Or do those ideas seem so far out of reach that the thought process then is: "*Why bother?*"

It's like they want to do just enough to get by, *nada mas*. To exist but not to thrive.

Being a somewhat socialist country, they are guaranteed their *alguinaldos* at Christmas and their government sponsored retirement funds so maybe they just see no reason to do anything more than just the bare minimum.

Which then I remember that the average income here is around $8,000 US annually. And I learn new things like how some of the more rural places in Costa Rica only got electricity a few years ago, and I have to keep reminding myself that they are so far behind the US.

Even though all the fast food chains can be found here and there are many modern conveniences, it is still developing in many ways as a country.

I mean, think about that for a moment - not having electricity. The US has had electricity since the 1800s when Edison developed mass power generation.

Again, it's now 2016 and some places in Costa Rica just got power a few years ago? (And who knows, there may be other places that I'm unaware of that still don't have it).

Until recently, some families in rural communities didn't have refrigerators much less laptops or cell phones. So...let me repeat that...no refrigerators. They lived off the land and prepared food on a daily basis. They cooked over wood burning stoves.

I may not have an oven right now in my current home but I can't imagine life without a refrigerator. And definitely not without a freezer.

Now, I think this is a choice. People in these rural areas could choose to move 30 minutes west and have electricity but for one reason or another, they don't.

I may try to live more simply but I need some basic modern conveniences. Where would my homemade vegan peanut butter and chocolate ice cream go, and how would I possibly make it without electricity for the food processor? Yes, I'm being a bit facetious here and no, I'm not asking for a vegan ice cream boutique shop to appear but really, electricity is a part of a life for most people around the world these days.

I don't know, I'm still trying to understand and assimilate. I can kind of understand how when the electricity goes out, or the water stops coming out of the faucet, or the bank line is out the door and around the block, you have no choice but to just say: *pura vida*. There's nothing that can be done. It happens all the time.

But I still don't understand why they've chosen it for their mantra... and fortunately, from articles that I've read recently, written by Ticos, there is a small culture shift happening and a recognition that maybe *pura vida* isn't all that it's cracked up to be... or it's lost its true meaning along the way, opening up the door for negative stereotypes like laziness and apathy to enter.

This is just the tip of the iceberg as to why it's challenging to live here, in the land of mañana. Sometimes I feel like I should just find a little hut on the beach surrounded by palm trees, with the ocean just a stone's throw away, and live a solitary life. That sometimes seems like it would be so much easier...and better.

Chapter 7
Oh machismo... you're just not needed

"My theory is that men are no more liberated than women."

Indira Gandhi

If I thought the States was male-dominated, well, it's nothing compared to Costa Rica. Even though there are some statistics that say Costa Rica has a high tolerance for women's equality, underlying that is still a society that is very much dominated by men and latin machismo. Here are a few great examples as to the extent of how much males are revered here.

When I adopted the kittens in 2014, a male *tico* friend came over and asked me if I was going to get the female fixed. Which of course I answered with, "*Yes, both of them!* " He was, to put it mildly, horrified. His response was, *"How could you possibly neuter the boy kitten?"*

When the Men's World Cup was happening in 2014 and Costa Rica's team made it into the playoffs, the country went wild. Businesses shut down, and big screens were set up in the main streets so everyone could gather together to watch the games. There were celebrations and parades after each game. The men's team, while they didn't end up going all the way, were welcomed home with fanfare.

In severe contrast, in 2015, the women's team made it to the World Cup Playoffs. There wasn't a single peep that could be heard in all of the country. Bars weren't playing the game, there were no big screen TVs on the *malecón* with tens of thousands of people taking the day off work and watching the games together. There were no parades, no celebrations, no lines of cars and pedestrians, honking their horns and yelling in the streets. Nothing. Not a single sound. I only knew about the games because friends in the US were talking about them online. When I asked *tico* friends why that was, I was told by many of them, *"Women shouldn't play futbol."* *Sigh*

When I was looking at a new apartment to rent, the property manager asked me to have sex with him. And not just once but multiple times and even via text message (which I have all the copies of). While I'm now used to this type of behavior and know how to handle it, this was a building that had both long term and short term rentals. In defense of single women who might be traveling and staying at the apartments, I informed the property owner, a man in the US, of what occurred. He told me: *"No one else has complained so I don't believe you."* Sounds like a man in the US in the 1950's, doesn't it?

But this was 2016. I told him I had all the text messages but he didn't care. He told me it's hard to find good managers and this one, while not great, did a better job than others. Oh, and did I forget to mention that the manager, when he was propositioning me for sex, had his wife in San Jose having his baby son? Literally, giving birth to his baby son just days before.

I had a friend in the States tell me that one of her friends just returned from a trip here, and she had met a guy who she was soooo happy with. They were now a couple, and she would return whenever she could. Hmmmm, yeah. I can almost guarantee you that same guy met another girl the week before, and a girl the week after she left, and all three of them think they are in some type of committed relationship. Most likely, he's also either married to a *tica* or has a *tica* girlfriend.

I know this from firsthand experience. It's happened to me many times. Sometimes I didn't know, and other times I knew but the guy would tell me that they were on a "break", or that when the girlfriend was in her home country, they were in an open relationship and free to see other people.

The guys here will tell you that they're single when really they have a wife, and probably a *tica* girlfriend as well. They may like you because they think you're a bit exotic, and because you probably have more money than them, and it's their old school machismo standards that they have to live up to for fear that they'll be "neutered" otherwise.

I even had one friend who, when I asked why he was with this other girl when he was trying to have sex with me, say: *"Chris, she's from Australia. You know how close Bali is to Australia? I want to surf Bali! And she can get me there. Plus, she buys me all kinds of new things like a phone, and a selfie stick and new clothes and shoes! And she takes me to really cool places, I get to surf wherever I want. I don't want to give that up. And again, she's my ticket to Bali!"*

So then I asked – why do you want to have sex with me?

His response was so very typical: *"Because she's been out of the country on her 90 day visa run and I'm kinda horny."* (Note: I never had sex with him)

Los Tres Guillermos

Ahh, the three Guillermos. I've changed their names but they did actually all have the same name, and so with friends, I had to give them nicknames so they could keep track of them all. Each of the Guillermos came into my life with the intention of wanting sex.

The first and the third both gave me the impression that they wanted more (and somehow, naively, I fell for it both times).

The second one, well, it was totally clear from the start that he just wanted to be "*amigos con derechos*". And honestly, out of the three, he was the one I appreciated the most. Probably because he wasn't lying to me, and we were both on the same page – I didn't want anything more from him either.

He was also the one with the girlfriend who spent half the year in her home country. It was the perfect arrangement. We'd go to each other's houses, make dinner, watch some TV, and then have our (very) fun romp in the sack. After that, we'd go our separate ways. It wasn't necessary to spend the night at each other's houses.

He came into my life rather unexpectedly. It started innocently enough (in my mind, at least). I had met him at the beach the year before and we had become friends, but I knew he had a "sort of, on again/off again" girlfriend.

Just days before our first hookup, I was writing down things that I wanted in my life. One of the main things that I missed from my California life was Sunday night dinners with friends.

And so, when Guillermo #2 texted me and asked me to come over for Sunday night dinner a few days after I wrote the list, I thought, "What a wonderful blessing from the universe." I had no intention of sleeping with him, I just thought we'd be sharing a good meal together. But after a few *Toñas*, one thing led to another and...

With the other two, it was a whole lot more complicated. Mainly because they were lying to me about their intentions and who they really were. And the sex in no way compared to that of the second Guillermo, so it wasn't even worth my time or energy.

Guillermo #3 I gave up on very quickly. His true colors showed up early on, and while I gave him a little bit more of a chance to prove otherwise, in the end he was what I would call, "a typical *tico*". Over the course of just a few weeks, we had exchanged more than 3,000 texts and then nothing but the sound of crickets outside my house. Literally. And all I had to show for the time together was a hickey.

The Typical *tico* is one who is all talk, no action. Guillermo #3 would post on Facebook, at least once a day, one of those "wisdom" sayings and quotes that you see shared a million times over. The topics ranged from God, to love, to friendship, to being a good person... But he didn't mean any of it.

This was just his online persona, the persona he wanted people to believe he actually was. And that's the problem with the typical *tico*. He says a lot but means none of it. His actions will never equal his words. I've found Ticos use the word "try" a lot but more often than not, they cannot ever truly make a commitment. They can't be truly authentic and present in their life.

I actually allowed Guillermo #1 to pop into my life on and off over the course of about 18 months. But eventually, while I did consider him a friend, it got tiring as there just wasn't any real substance. He tried to tell me he wasn't the typical *tico* who goes running home to his parents house every chance he got. But he was. And so every free moment when we could have been off playing together, he was with his mom and I was bored...on many levels. He tried to come over a few more times after I had ended it, but he eventually understood that I wasn't going to sleep with him and that if he wanted to be my friend (because technically, *friends with benefits* goes beyond just a booty call), then he'd have to show up for me more often and not just when it was convenient for him. I didn't want a relationship with him but I also didn't want to be someone's late night booty call. I don't know how many times I have to say it but... I'm not 16.

And then of course, there's *brahmacharya* to consider. The fourth *yama* in yoga's ethical guidelines concerns itself with the concept of sex and moderation. (Actually, in its truest sense, it says you're supposed to be celibate.) How can I embody the intentions of this beautiful yogic lifestyle, on and off the mat, if I'm off sleeping with Guillermo 1, 2 and/or 3?

When I started to reintegrate my yoga and mindfulness practice into my life, I did consider giving up "friends with benefits" sex all together. I realized it wasn't who I wanted to be, it's not how I wanted to show up in the world, and I definitely didn't want to be the other woman. (Or, in some cases, one of many women.)

At one point, I thought I had found the perfect man (my naivety often makes me laugh). A mutual friend had introduced us and we had gone out for dinner and drinks. It was the first intellectually stimulating conversation I had had in some time and was like a breath of fresh air in an otherwise dank, self-serving environment.

We talked for so long that he missed the last bus home so I offered to let him stay at my house, in the guest bed. He agreed, we went to my house, we talked more out on my terrace enjoying the night air and then went to sleep, in our separate beds.

Only when the morning came... he got up, came into my bed and tried to have sex with me! Seriously?! I would've understood if he had tried to sleep with me the night before as we were both a little buzzed, but to do so in the morning with a clear and sober head? I just don't get it. He didn't even say anything when he got into my bed. It was weird. And so very disappointing given the nice night we had had together.

He was, as it turns out, just another "typical tico".

I thought I'd learned all my lessons, that I was done with meeting men who only wanted to have sex with me. I thought I had put that chapter to bed and made it super clear to the universe that it was not something I wanted in my life.

But on my 40th birthday weekend, I met a nice guy. Atypical from what I normally go for, he wasn't the hot surfer with the amazing body. He was just your average guy with a nice smile. We chatted a bit, danced a bit, and he even sang me "happy birthday" in front of a crowd of people. We found each other on Facebook and that's when I learned that he had a girlfriend. Okay, no big deal. He was still a nice guy, someone who was local to where I lived, and potentially a new friend to hang out with.

I really do live in a fantasy land, looking back once again at those naïve thoughts.

He texted me one afternoon, saying it was a beautiful day and did I want to go out? I thought, *"Great idea! Where should we go and what should we do?"*

And the conversation went downhill from there...

He wanted to meet somewhere private. What was I wearing? What was I wearing underneath my clothes? He wrote he wanted to "steal a passionate kiss."

Not caring at this point, I scolded him, telling him that he had a girlfriend and how could he say these things to me? He just continued on...even telling me that maybe if I gave him the opportunity to go out with me, he'd change his mind about his long-term relationship and leave her to be with me.

Ick.

The next day, he continued to text me. At 6:30 in the morning, he sent me a message that said if we had gone out the night before, we would be waking up together now. Again, he said that maybe if we made love and felt the passion together, that he'd feel differently and leave his girlfriend.

I bluntly told him that I'm not an idiot, and would never do that, not just because he has a girlfriend but because I'm not some girl with low self-esteem who doesn't recognize that he'll do the same thing to me in the future.

Nausea had set in at that point.

And disgust.

I dropped this lying, cheating pig as a friend from Facebook and stopped responding to his messages. My property owner, a *Tica*, would have said, "*que cerdito*" (that little pig). That's what she had previously called the business owner who took off for his worldwide travels and didn't pay me for the two prior month's services before leaving. She was embarrassed that it was a *tico* who had such poor manners.

After deleting all traces of this *cerdito*, I texted the one *tico* friend who hadn't hit on me and told him I was grateful that he had never tried to have sex with me. Weird, yes. But I find myself having to find gratitude in strange places these days.

I could have also contacted the *cerdito's* girlfriend but I chose not to. I've done that once in the past and all it did was make the girl angry with me, after which she stayed with her boyfriend.

Sad, but true.

In this particular case, it's just not worth putting the effort into something that I know won't change. I'd rather put my energy elsewhere, where I can make a difference.

I'll admit that a part of me is fascinated by Costa Rica's male-dominated culture. It's like watching a train wreck - you can't look away. I know that I let the above situation go on for longer than it needed to, but I wanted to see how far he would go without me giving him any advances. The only texts I sent him were reminders he had a girlfriend and that only seemed to fuel him to continue.

I read a study that said out of 250 Costa Rican men, only three claimed to be faithful to their female partners. THREE. It's a small study, I'll admit, but that ratio says a lot about why relationships are so messed up here.

One time, an ex showed me a picture of a cute little African/Caribbean baby and said, "I want one just like that." I told him, "Well, that will be a little difficult with me unless we consider adoption." You know what he did? He found an African/Caribbean girlfriend. And he got her pregnant. It's not that he wants the girlfriend, he definitely doesn't want to get married or settle down (trust me, he still flirts with me when we talk on the phone), he just wants the cute little baby that his girlfriend can produce.

Really, I honestly have no interest in any of these men who hit on me. I love men, and I love sex, but I know too much about how they treat women to ever want to develop a healthy and loving relationship with any of them. If that was even a possibility. Which it probably isn't.

And if you didn't think the cheating was enough to totally discount these men...

They are also weirdly obsessed with their penises. I can't tell you how many penises I've seen since moving here. Not that I've slept with any of these men but they all like to take out their penis and show them to me. It's weird, really really weird. It's almost caveman like. I'm all prepared for some guy to come along one day, beating his chest and throwing me over his shoulder as he runs with me off into the jungle.

Knowing what you know now about the men here, I'm sure it doesn't surprise you that I've had some interesting propositions over the years

When I first moved to Tamarindo, one of my regular taxi drivers offered to marry me so I could become a legal resident. He said he didn't want anything from me, only to help me, as I'm such a nice person. *(Imagine me rolling my eyes here...they all want something)*

Then there was the night on the beach in Nosara. The moonlight was sparkling on the water, and I was making out with a cute surfer against a piece of driftwood when he whispered into my ear...let's make a baby. Well, that was a mood killer. I had to stop myself from laughing when I realized he was serious.

He proceeded to state his case. I would be such a good mom, and we'd have a cute baby and he would help out as he could. Maybe I could even live with his family. The thoughts running through my mind? *Oh my. What world am I living in?*

About a week later, I was out with another friend who also told me that we should have a baby together. What the hell? Was I giving off some type of pheromone in which men responded with wanting to have a baby with me?

I've also been hit on by every age range possible. I've had 19-year-old surfers try to have sex with me as well as 55+ year old men. With the 19-year-old, I just shook my head in disbelief. I mean, really?

Many of the girls here get pregnant in their teens so potentially, I could be older than his mother. I'm not going to say I wasn't flattered. A 19-year-old surfer with a rock hard body hitting on me? Sure, that feels great. But it's also so very wrong. And weird. At least to me. My *tico* friends here tell me that it's totally normal and acceptable for there to be large age ranges between partners.

Again, no. Weird and wrong.

One of my girlfriends here puts it so perfectly: *"Latinos will promise you the sky, the moon, and everything else for you!! If you are the right person, you will be the mama in the house but they will have tons of ladies in the bar."*

She also told me...
"Chrissy you need to learn...

CHRISSY GRUNINGER

No ticos, hahahah."

And then my housekeeper will tell you, "*Estar sola es fea.*" To be single is terrible. I think she's wrong however. At least here on the Rich Coast. To be single in Costa Rica is probably one of the best, most empowered decisions a girl can make in her life. I'll admit that having a man in the house to remove the wolf spider from the shower would have been a nice perk but, when I think about all the headaches that come with having a *tico* in your life...no thank you. I can take care of the gigantic tarantula-sized spider on my own.

On being single: It's a choice. I don't need someone else to validate who I am; I've never needed to fit into society's norms.

A part of me is quite sad about the accepted culture and relationships between men and women here. Not so much for me but for the other girls who get played, and for the men who can't seem to open their minds and hearts to a real, honest, committed relationship.

For the women, sometimes, I feel like they desperately need (in my opinion) a leader to speak up for them and make their voices heard. They are so much more than they are often given credit for. I secretly think about ways I can plant seeds to start a suffragette revolution here on the Rich Coast. I want to yell: *You are so much more than your body! You do not just exist to be barefoot, have babies, cook the meals and clean the house.*

You can do and be anything you want. Do more, be more, LIVE more!

And for the men…How miserable their lives must be, on an internal level for them to never feel satisfied or understand the great pleasure they can receive by trusting in, and loving, just one woman. It's probably something they don't even know exists.

Many *Ticos* who I've met don't seem to know how to truly love someone and have passion, friendship and connection. I was told once by a gringo that *Ticos* are all about "relationships", but it's not what I would consider normal, healthy or acceptable. Lying, cheating, manipulating. In my world: Not normal. Not healthy. Not acceptable.

Except here, it is. Here, that's the definition of a relationship.

Having an honest conversation about what's going on? That just wouldn't happen. They can't have honest conversations with themselves much less others.

I've known good, kind men who are terrified of the women they're with. Here's an example: one of them actually broke his commitment to drive me home one night (after sunset) because *his woman* would be at the beach and he couldn't risk trying to explain to her that he was trying to be nice and ensure that I got home safely from that day's activity. That she wouldn't believe he was literally just going to drop me off at my house, stay in his car and make sure I got the key in the door before driving away.

SIGH

It's all so sad to me. If that was my boyfriend, I'd be so proud of him for being concerned about another woman's safety.

But disempowered, insecure women are unable to see it that way.

The essence of language...

I wonder if some of the reason for their relationship issues, besides being a latin machismo society, is that Costa Rica, unlike nearly every other country in Latin America, chooses to use "*usted*" instead of "*tu*", when it comes to friendships and partnerships.

Both of these are forms of the word "you".

Usted, in most Spanish speaking countries, would be used in a formal conversation such as when a student speaks to a teacher or when addressing the President of the country. Here in Costa Rica, *ticos* use *usted* at all times and I'm often corrected when I use the word *tu*. I used to tell Troy, *"But we're together, we're a couple, I'm not going to use a formal salutation with you like you're a stranger or somehow not my equal."*

It's not just Troy who would get frustrated.

Many *ticos* have told me it actually offends them when people use the form *tu*. They say they'll put up with it by *gringos* even though they cringe inside when they hear it. They assume you're just making a mistake, however I intentionally use it. I don't care. I think it's offensive to talk with my friends like they're strangers. That would be like, instead of calling a friend by his first name, you greeted him with "Hello Mr. Garcia".

Using a formal salutation with your partner or with friends and family just feels wrong. And it makes me feel very disconnected from the person - like we can never develop a strong, supportive and real relationship because it will always be at arm's length.

In a somewhat surprising contrast, they also overuse the word "*mi amor*" (my love). Can you imagine going into a Cheesecake Factory or even a McDonalds and having the server who has just seated you or taken your order call you *mi amor*? Well here the server at the restaurant will call you *mi amor*. The guy at the veggie market will call you *mi amor*. The security guard who opens the door of the bank for you will call you *mi amor*. *My love* starts to lose any type of meaning when it's used all over the place and with total strangers.

Sadly, there is still the very real stereotype here that if you're a girl and aren't married with kids by the time you're 25 (and 25 is pushing it), then there must be something wrong with you.

It's why I've known *ticas* to get married to old retired *gringos* just so they can say they are married. (The "ewww" factor increases exponentially here.)

Speaking of marriage and the way females are seen here, this might be a good place to note that the word for "wife" in Spanish is *esposa*. The word for handcuffs is *esposas*. This is really quite mentally disturbing to me.

Another interesting word fact: "commitment" in Spanish is *compromiso*. Yes, I believe that compromises need to be made in relationships but I just don't understand how that's the word for commitment.

All that makes me wonder, do *ticos* actually know and understand what love is? What is their definition of wholehearted, authentic love? Which then begs the question...how can you be truly happy if you don't truly love?

Always trying to understand

I'm still trying to understand what the underlying issue is here. Yes, there's latin machismo. Yes, in general, women are oppressed. I can tell you that they had a female president but she had republican-style ideals, which possibly made her more respected by the men in the country.

I once had a few friends visit and as we walked around town, they asked me, *"Where are all the women?"*

It wasn't something I had taken much notice of before but when they brought to my attention the lack of females, I did realize they were right.

There are very few women who work in the businesses around town; most of the places I frequent have male employees.

Not to say there are *no* women, but in looking around, you notice that very few women work visible jobs. There are a lot of female housekeepers at private homes and at hotels, but the bank tellers, the restaurant servers, the front desk concierges, the tour guides and the hotel management teams do seem to have a lot more men than women.

Another friend and his wife remarked one day how there are so many young teenage girls walking around town, not in school, but with babies or toddlers in tow. They were right too. It's something I try not to think about, but when it's pointed out, it's all you can see.

It has to be difficult, to be a girl in this country. Their constant state of being jealous combined with a low self-esteem and very few empowered role models must be a terrible place in their minds (and body) to live. If it was just girls in their teens or early 20's, that would be one thing. I can admit that, while I was independent in my teens and 20's, I was also a tad insecure - most of us are at that age - but my insecurity lessened when I realized I didn't need a man to be fulfilled.

Here, again, if you're not married by the time you're 25, there's something wrong with you. It's okay if you're a man in his 30's, still living at home with mom who is doing your laundry and paying your cell phone bill, but if you're a single woman, that's not acceptable.

Countless times, I've had both *ticos* and *ticas* (with again, no filter) ask me why I'm single. Why am I not married? Why don't I have children? Every time I travel, staff at hotels ask me the same thing. It's such a foreign concept and they just cannot understand. And when I express my independence with closer friends, they often think I'm fighting with them. I've learned to laugh at the situation which only infuriates them more, as they just cannot understand why I would choose to be single.

I'll give you my reason but first, a quote from Frida Kahlo that truly explains it in just two perfect sentences:

"No quiero un amor a medias, rasgado, partido por la mitad. He luchado y sufrido tanto, que merezco algo entero, intenso e indestructible."

"I don't want a love, torn, split in half. I have fought and suffered so much, that I deserve something whole, intense and indestructible."

My reason?

I'm empowered as a woman and do not need to be a wife or a mom to define who I am. I don't need a man to feel fulfilled. Nor do I need children.

Yes, I've been told that I'd make a great mom, and that's nice to hear, that people think I'm a kind, loving person, but that doesn't mean I have to have my own children. Maybe I'll adopt. Maybe I'll foster. Maybe I'll find other ways to share the love that I have to give. It's not even so much that I don't want children, I just don't want to get pregnant, have the dad not be fully present in the child's life and be a single mom. That's the norm here. The norm is that dad gets mom pregnant and then disappears. Or cheats. Or solicits prostitutes (which is legal here). They may even be married but the wife is still considered a single mom and dad lives somewhere else - that's just their way of life, their story. But I don't want it to be mine. Or my child's.

Also, so many of the men and women here are looking for... well, I guess the best way to explain it would be a "sugar daddy" or "sugar mama".

I've seen both men and women here put on false faces and tell their *gringo/gringa* partners that they love them just to get something from them – a free place to live, free meals, gifts, a trip to the United States, free travel around the country and to other countries, etc.

It saddens me to see this. The *ticos/ticas* know what they're doing, the *gringos/gringas*, unfortunately, are often not aware that they are being taken advantage of. Many *ticos* are very good at pretending that their love is true. Most of the time, in these situations, the foreigners are older - at least five years, but often much, much older. And so many of them truly believe that the *tico/tica* is in love with him/her.

To me, lying and cheating are as bad as physical abuse, it just doesn't leave physical scars. Mental and emotional abuse are about control and power, having aggressive psychological domination over someone else.

And because the females are so disempowered, they're unable to understand that this way of life is not acceptable, appropriate or necessary. This isn't a cultural issue that I should tread lightly on, this is a humanity issue. I look at the children here and I feel sad that they will continue to grow up in a society that is so far out of balance, has so many insecurities, and such a diminished value of self-worth.

If I had to compare it to something in the States, I'd say living here is like living in a red state (which I suppose, after the 2014 and 2016 elections, there's a whole lot more of them now).

Growing up in California, I just didn't ever think about the inequalities that still exist in other states (and I'll admit, probably a few places in California as well). I was brought up to appreciate other cultures. I never noticed the color of someone's skin and thought negatively of them because of it. They just have more melanin is all I thought (and often-times I was jealous as it takes forever for my skin to tan).

As a woman, I never thought that I *couldn't* do something. I know I can pretty much do anything that I set my mind to.

I realize that in some places in the US, there still exists inequalities and prejudices. But I also think that those regions are out of the norm and so far behind the times. And that's how I see Costa Rica.

Costa Rica is kind of like a combination of several different eras in the US. It's the Wild West of the 1800's combined with the 1940's and 50's oppression of women, and then the free love and drugs of the 60's and 70's. My hope is they will become more progressive, but I don't know if that will happen in my lifetime.

It's one of the reasons why I have said that maybe I should go off into the forest and live like a monk, or whatever the female version of a monk is.

I suppose I should start researching that if I'm indeed going to attempt it someday.

I can honestly see myself in a little shack in the rainforest with the beach just a few steps away, living off coconut, mango and banana trees that surround my property.

Perhaps human interaction is overrated.

Having always been a very social person with plenty of friends, this is a relatively new concept for me, but one I'm seriously considering exploring.

Chapter 8
I'm Sure You've Guessed It By Now, Doing Business Here Sucks

"Perseverance is failing nineteen times and succeeding the twentieth."

Julie Andrews

When I was planning my move to Costa Rica, I had dreams of supporting local companies. I just had no idea that Costa Rica is considered one of the worst countries to try to do business in. Or what that actually meant.

I thought I'd come here, help the local businesses market themselves, reach more people, make new connections and increase overall awareness. I was excited for what I thought would be an amazing opportunity. I mean, really, it's super easy to market Costa Rica. All I have to do is show a picture of a monkey and people go wild.

Plus, I didn't want to be one of those people who just come to Costa Rica and sit around all day and do nothing to give back and support the country where I was living.

> I was ready and willing to show up and work hard to give back to the place I was calling home.
> But... Costa Rica and its culture of doing business had other things in mind...

Costa Rica is indeed known as one of the worst countries to do business in, and from what I can tell, the *ticos* are totally okay with that - they don't want their status to change.

Because of this, many foreigners choose to have illegal businesses here. They don't pay taxes to their home country and they don't pay taxes here – definitely a win/win for them as long as they never get caught. And from what I've learned from my own experiences, that approach truly is much easier than trying to run a legitimate business.

Of course, another option would be to not run a business and instead work in the existing local businesses. Many foreigners work illegally in restaurants and discotheques, tour companies and hotels, and make $3-5/hour.

That is not for me.

One main reason is because it would take jobs away from *ticos,* and the other is that my skills far outweigh being paid $3/hour. I think the last time I got paid $3/hour was when I was a pre-teen working for my mom at her pre-school during the summer months. And that was the minimum wage at the time.

Thankfully my skills put me in the position to run my own business but still I had clients who tried to take advantage of my time. I've had some who thought I was supposed to work for them 24/7, but I learned to just ignore their requests for immediate action.

I once had a client ask me to be his weekend office manager. He was going to pay me $20/day (Saturday and Sunday) to work for nine hours at the office and also be on call from 7 a.m. – 9 p.m. each day (so 14 hours for $20). Another company said they'd pay me $5/hour if I'd work six days a week, eight hours a day, which is sadly, the common work week and standard salary for locals in the hospitality industry.

Yeah, no. I've worked hard to learn and build my business, and my self-worth is so much higher than I suppose the majority of people here who would jump at the chance to work 48 hours a week and make a measly $240. So many people make a lot less with the minimum wage just $550/month.

In reality, when I was offered these small wages, I was angry. I have skills. I have not only a bachelor's degree but a graduate degree as well. I have multiple certificates in yoga studies and health coaching (and even one in wine studies but that's kinda useless here). I have attained extensive knowledge about online marketing, business management and strategy.

I've studied and worked hard in my life to develop the knowledge and abilities that I now use daily in my business. I know I deserve more and I'm not going to let anyone take that away from me. I've learned that for those clients who don't value my background or respect the work I do, it's their loss. Penny pinching and breaking down my work into dollars and cents is not acceptable.

So now it's time to share with you the story about the "cerdito" I told you about earlier... I had one business hire me to manage their social accounts. It was a temporary gig, just for three months, but it was a long three months. He was *tico,* with the typical mentality of only looking out for himself and not caring if he hurt others. The first month he didn't pay me because he was traveling in South America. The second month, he was in Europe. And actually, both times he was at home on the due date, but he'd tell me, *"Oh, there's just so much I have to do, I don't think I can take the time to get you paid"*. It takes two minutes to do an online bank transfer. You don't have two minutes!?

There was no reason not to pay me, he just made the decision that it wasn't necessary; he had priorities other than honoring our contract. I did the work, now I need to be paid.

It wasn't just me, however, he also didn't pay his housekeeper on time, sometimes going weeks without paying her and that job was her primary source of income. He just didn't care. It was all about him and what he wanted.

The worst part? Because I had sent him the invoices, I had to pay taxes on the income even though he *never* paid me!

This was the second time I worked with *ticos*. The other company would also not pay me on time. This "time" was not arbitrary, it was agreed to by a contract that we both signed.

One client actually tried to tell me that I had no respect for him or his culture. Honestly, it made me laugh and I just continued to respond in a loving, kind, but also firm way, which only infuriated him more.

He tried to tell me, in a very angry and somewhat abusive tone, that I didn't respect him or his country. It's not that I don't respect them - it's actually just the opposite - but the thing is, the respect has to be mutual. And paying me several weeks late is not respectful. If I paid my rent late, which was to a *tica* family, that would be disrespectful. And that would harm them as they have to pay their mortgage. They're providing me with a service and they need to be paid when we agreed payment would be made.

It's such a simple concept, no?

Another thing, both with gringos and ticos, there's no personal or professional responsibility to be had.

Here's how a typical conversation would go, now remember, this was with the owners of the company...

I would start by kindly and respectfully reminding them that payment for my services was overdue, and they would usually respond with some type of excuse. Then they would move into boasting... and then they would complain...

And that just wasn't about payment. Every time I sat down with them, they'd go through the same series of excuses, boasting and complaining. Not necessarily about our work together but about anything that was happening in their life.

For me, making excuses equals less trust and respect. Excuses, boasting and complaining make people appear weak, insecure and unable to accept responsibility, and lacking in integrity.

But getting back to his comment about living in his country and not respecting their ways...I would have to disagree. I didn't tell him this because he wouldn't have listened, but I do respect his country and that's why I ran a legal business here. I hired *ticos*, I paid taxes, and I'm (still) waiting on my residency. I also respect anyone in the US who is a foreigner and doing the same thing there.

It comes down to simply being respectful - Humanity 101 - to treating others as you would want to be treated. And if you're not going to honor your commitments, then that is not being respectful.

That would be considered selfish.

The last email I sent him simply said: "Blessings to you, may you be well". Again, my kindness probably just confused him and may have sent him off the deep end, leaving him even more incensed, but I stayed on higher ground. I could've retorted with everything I wrote above, or even threatened to sue (which he encouraged me to do), but instead it was more important to recognize that he obviously has his own demons, that he is in pain and suffering, and the only thing I could offer him was kindness.

Which is a good segue to... Hiring people to work with me also had its headaches and heartaches. Lots of them.

I absolutely loved the work they did...when they decided to do it.

Again, it's an issue of respect and professionalism, both of which are severely lacking here in the land of mañana. They just can't see beyond themselves and what they want. If the surf is up, work won't get done. If there was a big fiesta the night before, work won't get done. If they decide to take a last-minute trip, even though there is a set deadline, work won't get done. It doesn't matter to them if it hurts me, the business, and the clients we serve. Their actions suggest that they really don't care.

> The heartache came from knowing how smart these people were and yet, again, they just didn't care about improving themselves or supporting my company.

Often time, it comes down to...

They only work when they absolutely need to.

If they have enough money to get through today, then they don't need to do the work they've been contracted to do.

Take the example of one of my housekeepers. Sometimes, she just didn't show up. She didn't call. She didn't text. She thought it was okay to not clean my house on the day that we've designated, the day that I had set aside in my schedule to be home and have her come to my house. But if she happened to have money that day, then she didn't need to work.

They only work when they absolutely need to.

It's a selfish act and it hurts others yet they're oblivious. Just like Tico Time. From their perspective, they're living in the moment (*pura vida*), but living in the moment doesn't have to mean that you hurt others in the process.

Mindless versus mindful

Living in the present moment *actually* means that you're still mindfully aware of the actions you're taking and their resulting effects.

You cannot be mindfully aware and living with intention, if you are constantly hurting others and disregarding your commitments. Living in the present moment means you appreciate the moment but you must also fulfill your promises - to yourself and others. It's not about being selfish, it's just the opposite really. I'm not saying you have to be 100% altruistic all the time, but you also can't be 100% selfish. There needs to be a balance.

For many, living in the moment means they can do whatever they want because there was no yesterday and there is no tomorrow. In this mindless philosophy, they don't let things linger. If you have a disagreement today, by tomorrow they've moved on and it's no longer an issue. It may still bother you, especially if nothing was resolved, but for them, they're not giving it a second thought.

I'll admit that sounds a bit like Buddhism and letting go of attachments and feelings around an end result, but not if it's done without mindfulness. They aren't mindful about the harm they are causing and will even sometimes try to put the blame back on others, as if somehow it's another person's fault for their inability to hold up their end of an agreement.

I was once told by a *gringo* contractor that I had to dumb it down (his words, not mine) for the people I was working with at that particular company - that they were still operating in the early 20th century. He also explained to me that, *"yes - they were indeed sexist...and racist...and I was getting a double whammy as a white female."*

Here's the thing: I can't dumb it down.

Not just on principle but also because it would make me look weak as well as mindless. I've already got a negative mark against me for being a woman, I will not play into their stupid rules. I have a voice. I will be heard.

I'm an independent, confident women with a strong work ethic who is not intimidated by other people. I'm a woman who is efficient and who does the work you give me to do. I do it. If I can't do it, I will tell you. I know how to communicate. I know how to say no. I know how to say yes. That is both intimidating and scary for many of the *ticos* who I was working with at the time. And, it would appear, for *gringos* who've lived here for an extended period of time as well.

Life lessons

I've learned how to say NO here.

As an independent contractor, AKA solopreneur, I get to make my own decisions. I get to dictate when my work gets done and when I start and end my day. But not everyone understands this.

One employee of a client not only tried to tell me what my job was, he even went so far as to try to dictate my schedule and the actual hours that I would do the work (when what he was asking for was *not even in the contract*). He was in no way my supervisor nor had he any real power over me or my position with that company. But he sure thought he did!

As a solopreneur, I can play hooky whenever I want. I get to choose who my friends are and with whom I work. Who I want to associate with, who I want to have on my team. Every day is a free day. I get to work any day that I want and take off any day that I want. There are no more bad Sundays spent dreading Mondays, or dying to get to Friday. Every day for me is a Saturday.

I've always been pretty self-assured and confident, but being an entrepreneur requires another level of confidence. Especially in the bewildering upside down land of *mañana*.

I know I need to have humility, grace, and gratitude AND I need to be seen as a leader, and respected and valued.

I thought I was resilient before becoming an entrepreneur in Costa Rica but my capacity for resilience has gone through the roof. Seriously, it's shot up tenfold. And I'm more confident than ever that I'm making the right choices, even when deals go sour, because I learn from them and know what not to do, or what to do better, next time.

I've learned that not everyone is going to like me. And that's totally okay.

My inner voice doesn't berate or bring me down, it helps lift me up. It reminds me that I already have everything that I need. That's why, when things go awry, I can laugh. I'm not laughing out of nervousness, I'm laughing because other people think I should be scared and I just think the whole thing is crazy. That inner voice, it tells me that all is well and that I'll be taken care of (and no, I'm not actually hearing voices).

It's definitely a challenge to be a solopreneur in one of the most difficult countries to do business in. It's taken time and effort and a lot of hard choices to finally get to a comfortable point in my professional life. And it's still evolving and changing in each moment.

I use my yoga practice off the mat as much as possible when it comes to making choices in my business, remembering the yamas and niyamas and also understanding that not everyone has the same principles or understanding of greedlessness, selflessness and mindful living.

But I still need to show up, as me, walk my talk and live my values. I learned that those who understand that and can appreciate it are the ones with whom I want to work.

Chapter 9
Real on the Rich Coast Reflections: the Good... and the Not-So-Ideal

"Your hand opens and closes, opens and closes. If it were always a fist or always stretched open, you would be paralyzed. Your deepest presence is in every small contracting and expanding, the two as beautifully balanced and coordinated as birds' wings."

Rumi

Okay, so after all that, you may be asking yourself the question...why do I choose to live here? A very good question and one that gets asked of me quite a lot, actually.

Let me take a moment here to regroup with you all and share some more of the day-to-day moments... the complex and messy parts as well as the beautiful.

Now that I'm living here and not traipsing from one luxury eco-hotel to the next, I've seen a much bigger picture of the Rich Coast. I've seen homes with dirt floors, no glass or screens in the windows and rusty tin roofs. I actually live in a very typical home now, although thankfully I do have a tile floor.

Looking back to when I first arrived, it was like I woke up one morning in a foreign country and all my modern conveniences had just disappeared. Poof. Just like that. No dishwasher. No garbage disposal. No dryer, no car, not even yellow lemons.

I had thought, in California, that I was very much an "eco" kind of girl, but not until everything was taken away from me did I realize there was so much more I could do to truly live a sustainable existence.

Much of this lack of comfort was forced upon me, but I do consciously make some of the choices.

And, of course, the bottom line is... *I've chosen to live here.*

Now in the day-to-day reality, I start to forget things that were once so normal, like getting mail every day. Or really, any mail...period. There is no mail. There are no mailboxes. There are no street names or house numbers.

Like the visitor who thought Quepos was ghetto, the razor wire that lines the tall concrete walls between homes has become normal for me, it's where I want to be. It's no longer a scary sight resulting in me thinking I'm in some Central American version of the projects in South Central Los Angeles.

Sitting for hours on end in the freezing cold bank to make a deposit is also normal. I stopped asking the question: *"Why is there no option to deposit a check at the ATM outside?"* And I don't even bother with the question of, *"But can't I just make a deposit by taking a picture of the check with my smart phone?"*

When I got an email from my US credit union with the subject line: *Deposit a Check In Minutes!* you could literally hear me sigh. My mantra when dealing with Costa Rica institutions has become: *Don't ask why.*

Another ongoing problem, having consistent and fast internet. When I downloaded the newest version of Evernote, it told me: *"It will only take a minute."* Hah, yeah, for someone in the US that would be true.

There are no doorbells. If you stop by someone's home, you say, "*Upe?*" It's kind of like, "Hello, anyone home?" as you're peering into their house.

In some ways it's sweet but having been robbed twice, it can be a little creepy.

Everything that we (those of us from North America) would consider normal in our daily lives doesn't exist here. I need to repeat that: normal does not exist. Not our version, at least. I'm constantly having to repeat that to myself in order to maintain my sanity. Costa Rica has its own version of normal and it's not just 50+ years behind the United States, it's also crazy, backwards and upside down. But again, it's what's normal for them. They don't know any other way.

I'm trying to learn to accept the simplicity of this country and I have good and bad days. I have days when I want to cry because I just spent $22 on some cashews (which thankfully, I can now find) or $10 for a small box of healthy cereal. It still makes me a little crazy that the only time I can buy kale is at the weekly farmer's market.

Why doesn't anyone eat greens here!?!

On the bright side, unless it's Christmas week or *Semana Santa* (Easter week), there are hardly any cars or tourists walking or driving around where I live. There's no traffic or noise pollution except for the natural sounds from the jungle, which I like. There aren't even stop lights and stop signs are few and far between.

It's a much slower pace of life in which I can just sit outside on my terrace and watch the day go by. "Exciting" things happen sometimes, like the day that helicopters flew over our neighborhood and all the neighbors came out of their homes to see what was happening.

That's about the extent of what happens here.

In the more rural areas, "Monday morning traffic" might be a herd of cows walking on a dirt road. In the rainy season, as I wrote earlier, you may have to wait for the rain to subside in order to be able to cross the river, or if it's raining hard, the road itself will become a river and again, you learn patience while waiting out the storm on the side of the road.

At my local hardware store (which, by the way, is not open on Sunday's and closes at noon on Saturday's), there are no computers with which to do price checks. The employee will pull out "books" made of thick metal sheets that have been bound together, and which contain each item in the store and how much it is. As prices change, they use masking tape to cover up the old cost and write the new.

You also cannot walk through the hardware store aisles. You have to go up to the counter and ask the man (yes, always a man) for whatever it is you need and have him bring it to you. Then you walk to a different section of the store where a woman (yes, usually a woman) is behind a glass partition and rings up the sale.

The pet store (which is all of about 100 square feet) is inside the hardware store. And usually it's out of what you need. I'm often told, "next week" or "15 days". Except it's not really because they never bothered to order the item and are just hoping you'll either forget or won't return! I repeat again, the land of *mañana*.

There are no Reese's peanut butter cups or yellow lemons. When Troy and I would travel, I once made the comment that I'd like a yellow lemon in my water. He said yes, that was a lemon (pointing to the green lime floating in the glass). I said no, I wanted a yellow one. He continued to tell me that it was the same. What I didn't realize is he had no idea that yellow lemons existed and he couldn't understand why I kept asking for one when there was already a green lime in my water.

There's a guy that walks through the neighborhood every morning at 6:30 yelling "*Pancito!*" And a truck that drives through the community announcing, "*Huevos!*" over a loudspeaker. There's another guy that walks through the community with bottles of honey. A few times a week, someone will drive by with fruits and veggies. In summertime, there is an ice cream truck, and in town, there are the guys with their little carts selling fresh coconut water and yelling "*Pipa Pipa!*"

You ride in the front seat when taking a taxi. My friend laughed at me the first time she saw me get out of a taxi from the back seat. She asked me... *"Chrissy, do you think you're a celebrity?"*

You don't get bills here. You just have to remember to pay. Or if you happen to be at home when taxes or utility bills are due, there is another truck that drives through the communities with a loudspeaker reminding everyone when to pay. (Remember, there's no mail and no online billing and email notifications – probably because many people don't have personal computers.)

Another truck will drive through the community to let you know that the water or electricity will be turned off for maintenance the following day.

The typical houses that *ticos* (and I) live in are very simple and small. They generally do not have any closets, cabinets or drawers. They'll often also have the most uncomfortable furniture you've ever sat on. You'll be able to feel the springs in your bed's mattress, and your sofa won't have any seat cushions.

Some homes have no hot water. Mine included. I feel like my dishes (and my body and my clothes) are never fully clean. What I wouldn't give for a dishwasher! And sometimes the water just stops coming out of the faucet or showerhead, which is really not fun when you have a head full of shampoo lather.

Many people don't have cars and if they do, they're normally used, not new. Walking, buses, motorcycles, bikes and taxis are the most common forms of getting around.

I won't use the "*collectivo*" taxis as I've had friends tell me that bad things can happen – a *collectivo* taxi is when a random driver picks up multiple people - who don't know each other - along the road and then the fare is less per person. That just doesn't seem safe to me. I don't mind paying an extra few dollars for a taxi if it means I maintain my sense of personal safety.

Many people often stay in the town where they're from and don't explore or visit other areas of the country, besides San Jose. This is especially the case in the rural areas where many of them have never traveled past the next town over.

The average income here is $8,000 per year. That's about $650 a month. Mull that one over for a bit in your head.

Being from the United States, I've always had the luxury of being able to order anything I want...from anywhere in the world...and it just arrives on my doorstep. That's not the case here. Much to some of my friends' shock and amazement, there is no Amazon.com here. No Macy's. Not even a Target. The lifestyle of instant gratification - ordering something one day to have it delivered to your front door step the next day - is totally taken for granted in the United States. And if I'm being totally honest, there are days when I truly miss that way of living. It just doesn't happen here.

If you're lucky, you might be able to call up a store in San Jose and have them put the item on a bus, and then you have to go to the bus station to pick up the item (which may or may not have your name or any other identifying marks on it). But first you have to find the store, make sure they actually have the item, and then realize (and cry a little) that you're paying at least twice as much compared to what you would have paid in the States.

Overall, it would seem that many people here are living but not thriving. They're surviving. They do what is necessary to put food on the table that day. They're also grateful though. Any time I ask,

"How are you?" Many will respond with, "*Bien, qué dicha*", which means, "Good, fortunately".

They take time to linger, they take siestas, and they enjoy their life from what I can tell.

It's just not how I want to live my life. I want to enjoy my life and live simply, but I also want to do a whole lot more.

This compassion and understanding, as well as finding a balance and living life on my own terms, is an ongoing path. I stumble and fall all the time. But I do my best to remain on the path as that's what's truly important to me. It's what I believe in and what I believe will make the world a more beautiful place.

Edward Everett Hale said, *"I am only one; but still I am one. I cannot do everything; but still I can do something; and because I cannot do everything, I will not refuse to do the something that I can do."*

There is good and not-so-ideal everywhere in the world. I'm learning to not just accept but embrace it all – choosing to show up as my best self possible and live wildheartedly in a very imperfect world...

Chapter 10

Swimming Upstream In The Land of Mañana

"Remember, a dead fish can float down a stream, but it takes a live one to swim upstream."

W.C. Fields

At this point, on the precipice of shifting from my lost self to being found, I took some time to pause and be present with what *was* and *is*. What I wanted. And what I didn't want. All of which still holds true today.

As my fingers started typing away, I chose to switch out many of the passive *I want's* to more declarative-like statements. Both to acknowledge that so much of what "I wanted", I actually already had as well as to mandate to myself, the universe, whoever... that this was how I was choosing to show up and live my ONE beautiful life.

Here's what I wrote...

Looking back on the first few years of living here and feeling lost, I can see that I was choosing to swim upstream, against the current. While I actually believe it's good to swim upstream in life, I can also recognize that during those years, I wasn't always doing it in a mindful way. Kicking and screaming in a figurative sense would be a better analogy.

No wonder I felt so exhausted and disheartened in body, mind, heart and spirit.

Coming to this realization, I can mindfully acknowledge that I don't want to fall into the typical lifestyle here, be it *gringo* or *tico*. I have to create a balance of the two –the middle way – and then go beyond that.

I am free...

To travel on this journey of life with clarity, ease and harmony. I know, that's not always how life works, there are always going to be stormy skies and potholes in the road (here especially, literally and figuratively).

My goal is to learn how to accept those challenges and to come out an even better, more mindful, more lovingkind person. Sure there are days when I feel like I've got a dark cloud hovering over my head and following me around, wherever I go. I choose to see that dark cloud and I not only make my own rainbow but the resulting treasures as well.

Ultimately, I choose to strive for balance in love, in health, in what I choose to eat and how I manage play time, work time, and me time.

Lacking worries about the past and having faith in the future...I take care of myself, in the present.

There is sunshine, blue skies, and time spent in the fresh air. There are stormy afternoons spent swaying in a hammock.

I work with good, long-term clients who respect and value the work that I'm doing and I hire team members who are knowledgeable, respectful and responsible.

I choose to make time on the mat: yoga, breathwork, meditation, stretching (preferably free from cockroaches...who also seem to love my yoga mat and mysore rug when they're rolled up).

I then take my yoga practice off the mat to be reflected in every word I speak and action I take.

I am love. I have ongoing commitments to friendships and personal relationships.

There is security in my daily life - both a safe home as well as an abundance of funds in my bank account.

I have a healthy glow to my skin and a fit, strong body.

I have Sunday night dinners with friends, sex in a committed loving mature relationship, time for my personal projects, and income to be able to do the things I enjoy, like travel and cooking compassionate meals. Or even just a buy a car to take a road trip as summer never ends here and it's always best to appreciate the moment.

I feel fully alive and choose to associate with others who also want to swim upstream in a mindful, heartfelt way.

The people I know here may say they feel alive in their daily life as they do coke and ecstasy, drink, or just waste away their days sitting on the beach, but that isn't how I choose to live my life.

I still desperately seek intelligent conversations in person free from gossip, negativity, and worry.

I choose to seek out people who agree with me but also challenge me. I have that with friends in the States but it's different. An online connection, while potentially still strong, is not the same as human contact and interaction. It's the in-person *sangha* that I'm craving, and that which is sorely lacking here.

I'm putting these desires, my goals, out to the universe, right here, right now.

Living here, I don't want to feel like I'm on a permanent vacation. I loved *loved* **loved** Spring Break when I was in high school. But I don't want that to be my everyday experience and so many of the people in the beach communities are on a permanent Spring Break. That's their daily life. And it's just not for me.

For me, it's an illusion; it's not real life.

It is said in Buddhism, *"to live one's life, the question is can we accept the ten thousand joys and beauties of life and the ten thousand sorrows and losses and griefs?"*

So many people here can't. They can face the joy but not the sorrow. They are mindlessly swimming with the stream (AKA status quo), rather than choosing to mindfully go against the current and live a meaningful life on their own terms.

I am intoxicated with life. Just life. Nothing external needed, nothing needing to be internally consumed. I feel every moment and I hear, taste, smell, touch, and see each experience, whether they are good, beautiful, and passion-filled moments, or full of sadness, pain and fear.

And I choose to go even beyond that, to develop my inner knowing, my inner self – Svadhyaya, in the yoga sense – in order to create more harmony in myself and in the world.

I go deep into my spirit, the essence of who I am, and feel every moment, every breath. I choose to be with open-hearted loving beings, and know other people on that same level.

I respect and appreciate our differences.

I choose not just to exist, but to live. Live fully. Live freely. Thrive, and feel, and be in every moment, accepting that what I have is all I need.

If new people or things come into my life, I can decide if I want to accept them or let them go.

I must also accept and respect that the people here, the ones who don't live a life that I can condone or desire, are living their lives. This is THEIR life.

Do I wish that we could all be further along on the path?

Yes...that is one of my greatest desires - that others will wake up to this ONE beautiful life and get out of living a monotonous, bland, meaningless and numb existence. To make mindful choices, from the simple to the complex... to have both self-respect and respect for others, think beyond themselves, and see the bigger picture.

I was brought up to always see the good in people. And I suppose over time, and over many painful heartaches from friendships and partnerships gone bad, that belief has diminished and my own core self has hardened. I can see that in myself and I'm slowly chipping away at that wall, to be open-hearted towards all.

But at the same time, I must learn that there's a difference between being present and open-hearted versus being taken advantage of and manipulated. And I must be mindfully aware that both will present themselves to me and look very similar, but with very different results.

When we choose to mindfully swim upstream, change happens. We're consciously choosing to shift, to challenge the status quo, to create a different set of rules compared to society's norms and make our own path while acknowledging the choices of others along the way.

At the heart of it, I must continue on my path of mindfully swimming upstream.

To take pauses when needed. To always stand up for what I believe in. To be a role model, all the while knowing that I, too, will probably fall off the path at times. Whether I'm pushed down or I fall down, I must always pick myself back up, brush myself off and keep moving forward and upward.

My hope is that others will also choose a mindful path to walk on – to make their own authentic, wildhearted path – continuing to move forward, with no delusion or denial.

To choose to do more, be more, learn more, give more, love more and live more.

What a beautiful place the world would be.

Acknowledging the good, the not-so-ideal *and* that I was making a conscious choice to swim upstream in the land of *mañana* was how I finally found myself back on the path of mindful living, remembering that my Inherent Harmony already exists within me.

Still, there was much more work to be done...

LOST AND FOUND IN THE LAND OF MAÑANA

PART 2: FOUND

LOST AND FOUND IN THE LAND OF MAÑANA

Chapter 11
Introduction

"I wanted a perfect ending. Now I've learned, the hard way, that some poems don't rhyme, and some stories don't have a clear beginning, middle, and end. Life is about not knowing, having to change, taking the moment and making the best of it, without knowing what's going to happen next. Delicious ambiguity."

Gilda Radner

"How are you not a raging alcoholic?"

"How have you not gone off the deep end?"

"How can you possibly live in that country? You should come home."

These concerns and others like them resound in my ears from worried stateside friends and family on a regular basis.

The question beneath all of them, however, is: How can I possibly put up with not just the culture shock and inability to get my favorite items, but also the burglaries, racism, sexism and other negative-isms that permeate the spirit of this beautiful country.

My answer is always the same. I'm healthy.

"But seriously, Chrissy, come home. It's not worth living in such a... place."

Yes. It is. Really. But it's about finding a way to live here that makes sense, for me. It's about fully embracing the storm overhead and creating the rainbow. I've always been a realist. And I know that rainbow isn't just going to appear – I have to make it.

Yet for all the insistence from some that I return to the States because of the inconvenience and danger, there are others who have told me that I'm not allowed to complain because I get to live in Costa Rica.

They envy my life and wish that they were on the beach sipping tasty adult beverages, as they assume that must be what life is like in paradise. All the time.

This sentiment really makes me laugh... and wonder how anyone could maintain such a perspective (even if they haven't read my books and blogs and gotten a fuller picture of the reality of living here).

Seriously, who doesn't know that the grass is not greener on the other side? Well, except perhaps literally. We do get a lot more rain and our environment does indeed stay more green than other places in the world. But figuratively, no. The saying exists for a reason.

Grass (like most things) looks better from a distance because then you can't see the flaws. But get right up close and you'll see weeds and scorched patches. No matter how lush it looks from 20ft away (or 3,000 miles), my lawn is just the same as yours.

Life is all about what you make of it. And I absolutely refuse to pretend that there are unicorns spewing cupcakes because I live in what everyone thinks of as paradise.

(By the way, cupcakes don't even exist here, just like yellow lemons!)

My green grass, AKA my life, is a patchwork — an ecosystem made up of greens and browns, weeds and bugs and wildflowers thriving harmoniously.

In that ecosystem, there is a delicate balance where everything, the sublime *and* the gross/icky/irritating, is essential. For me, this is paradise... for the sole reason that I'm healthy.

But that doesn't mean that bad things don't happen or that I don't find a way to cope. I've got an awesome pair of big girl pants and I'm not afraid to wear them.

Given everything, do I still love it here?

Of course! I've got summer year round and macaws flying against the backdrop of a blue sky while monkeys eat mangoes lazily in a nearby tree.

Between nature, my good health and my inherent harmony (which I lost for a while but am slowly getting back), I have managed to stay sane. That is why I stay and what creates the rainbow – the light and the dark, the good and the bad, the yin and the yang.

Balance.

And 99% of the time, I am barefoot.

Have I mentioned how important that is to me? Let me just say again. That is *super* important to me.

I wasn't always balanced however. When I finally came back to being me, I could look back at the first few years and see that I was lost. So very lost. I wasn't taking care of myself. I wasn't practicing my yoga, on or off the mat. At least, not in the wholehearted way that I normally did, when I lived in what I considered "normal".

When I finally came to the realization that I was lost, things started to show up in my life to help me find my way back.

One of the major imbalances I noticed was that I no longer had a community of open-minded, innovative people to surround myself with. I couldn't drive down to Spirit Rock in the lovely Marin hills and attend a day long workshop on Buddhist philosophy, talk with others about what we were learning and soak up the information to apply to my life.

I started looking around for Buddhist communities but still have yet to find one near me. There are a few, up north and in San Jose. I thought of starting one on my own. I even put out some feelers to local people.

But then I just shook my head, no.

That wouldn't work either. I wanted to be around people who were living their yoga/spirituality/beliefs/values, every day.

I'm not judging others who want to go out and get wasted, drive drunk, use cocaine, etc etc. I respect everyone's right to choose what they want in their lives.

I also respect my ability to choose not to invite certain energy into my inner circle. My spiritual geography has boundaries which tourists aren't allowed beyond. (That helps with the sanity.)

Jim Rohn once said that *"we are the sum of the five people we most often associate with."*

I wholeheartedly believe that is true, which leads me to be infinitely more conscientious about those who get the bulk of my time and energy.

I don't feel that everyone needs to be at my level or ahead of me. I can certainly serve as a role model. I've also got a long way ahead of me, fortunately with amazing people who I can look up to for support.

However, for those who haven't even started down the path, or have no desire to live what I like to call an authentically happy, healthy and harmonious life, I have learned to minimize my time cultivating relationships.

I choose to create community with those who want to show up and do good things in the world, whatever that may be for them.

I now know how easy it is to get lost when you're hanging out with people who don't challenge themselves to show up as the best and most authentic version of themselves. They can't offer that challenge to you and it can be easy to get distracted and pulled off course without people actively invested in your growth as a being.

Of course, who I spend time with is my choice and responsibility and I fully understand my ability to share my path to happiness and fulfilment with others in the hopes that it might resonate with them.

Right now though, I'm just trying to stay on the path, doing my best to move forward. I choose not to hang out with people living unhealthy lives because I want to do more with my life.

The reality is that my happy, healthy and harmonious choices put me in a very difficult predicament.

There are very few people who I can associate with here and continue on my path of living a happy, healthy and harmonious life. Which means I don't go out much or socialize - in person.

Like my friend told me, if I don't drink or use drugs, it'll be next to impossible to make friends here.

It's delusional for me to think the day to day culture here will change based upon my preferences. Therefore, I have to accept the circumstances and make the most of it.

As cynical as it sounded, I couldn't deny that my Psych 101 professor had a point when he wrote on the black board our first week of class: *People don't change.* He wasn't 100% right, but he also wasn't 100% wrong.

From my personal experiences, I would amend the statement to say:

People don't change until they really want to.

I had to be honest with myself that the only one craving a change was me, in which case, I had to work with what I could control - me.

This next section of the book includes the words of my soul: my body, mind, spirit and heart. It's my story of re-finding my Inherent Harmony. I now know myself, what's important to me and what I value more so than ever before.

Looking back I took so many risks... and failed. And failed. And failed. I never stop trying, though. I never stop believing. For me, life is about trial and error. I fall down, I pick myself back up.

If I didn't try, I would remain stuck in neutral. Paralyzed. Fearful of doing, well, anything. I admit that sometimes I take on situations with a pretty good chance of failure, simply to see if I can't beat the odds. If I don't at least try, I can't know what I'm capable of, let alone innovate and take things to the next level. My failures are nothing less than stepping stones to success.

Whenever possible, I learn my lessons and move on, forgoing obsessing about "what could have been"...in life, love, and even work. Sometimes I might become melancholy but then I dig into my spiritual toolbox and work to create a shift in my perspective to help me snap back to the present.

My mantra is:
This is where I am now. This is where I want to be. One way or another, I will make it work.

This, I have accepted, is the new normal. I've made choices and implemented steps that have made being disappointed a lot less likely.

I've let go of being in control (well, most of the

time!).

I've been a lot more honest these last few years about who I am and what I want. Disruptive people, places, things...none of that enters my life these days - at least to the degree that I can prevent it. I have no desire to live in drama. It may make me seem anti-social at times but I make no apologies about choosing what is best for me and in line with my life goals. My time is valuable and I don't want to waste it on frivolity or superficial fluff.

As a result of doing what I need to do for myself, I've been able to slow down and enjoy moments as they happen. I notice the little yellow butterflies flying around my terrace and the location of the sunset changing as it moves with the seasons. I watch as squirrel monkeys play with each other on my drying sheets.

I'm even more resilient than before. The more this country threw at me, the more strength I had to find in myself to work through it. I bounce back a whole lot faster now and those doors of opportunity keep opening.

The unknown is no longer a scary place but rather a place to explore, to lean in and see what awaits me.

Often just the act of stepping outside of my comfort zone, allowing my light to shine in the darkness, scary though it might feel in its infancy, is all that is needed to illuminate my path and make my next steps clear.

That's simply not something in my power when I choose to live in a state of fear. If I was too afraid of the unfamiliar to move forward, I'd end up moving back to the States as so many people have suggested.

I love myself far too much to let fear win and send me back to daily runny noses and all of the other physical ailments I endured in California. My choices now all have a very singular aim; get behind me fear, I seek my inherent harmony. I live outside of my comfort zone.

When I came across the word sanguine, everything made perfect sense. It was the perfect word to describe how I feel (and what many people don't understand about me or my life): *Contentment in chaos. Empowered to thrive in an imperfect world.*

I have found a way to be happy, fulfilled, to live out my purpose and create a wildhearted life.

I have found contentment amongst all the chaos and daily struggles that would normally suck the life blood out of most anyone.

Sanguinity is similar to resilience but for me, it's deeper. It's how I keep centered, inspired and motivated to do, be, give, learn, love, and *live* more.

It keeps me showing up every day, doing my work. I've learned how to say No when I can see that saying Yes would only create more chaos. This understanding that it's my responsibility to thrive, even in an imperfect world, is how I remain focused on my goals and present along the journey to get there.

When I was still living in California, I could have focused on the 3000+ miles that was between me and Costa Rica. That distance, in itself, could have overwhelmed me and caused me to give up.

That's why sometimes, you just have to keep envisioning the goal itself, rather than the distance to it. I could let the distance psych me out, but then where would I be? In order to get from A to B, I had to prioritize me, my needs and wants.

The journey of self-discovery is absolutely crucial in creating a harmonious life. My true essential nature includes all of me, beyond just being a female, mom to two adorable kittens, sister, daughter, friend.

It also includes my individuality, innate skills and traits, values, ethics, and principles. I choose to focus on my strengths and either work on my weaknesses or realize that's not where I thrive and move on.

When I show up as my best possible self, I know I can inspire and motivate others, yet another thing I can't do when I find myself trapped by fear or trying to live someone else's version of *my life.*

During the time I spent lost and distracted, I found myself wholly disconnected from such a goal.

So I created an outline for the life I wanted to lead. I asked myself:

What steps do I need to take?

What will I do? How will I serve? Who will I

work with (who won't I work with)?

What type of nourishment will I provide my body, mind, spirit daily, weekly, yearly?

What toxins are in the way? What is preventing me from living this beautiful life that I've outlined?

What am I committed to today? How will that get me to where I need to be?

The main question always is: How can I live my life as an example to others?

When we open up our hearts, when we are our authentic selves, we heal that which has been harmed, love ourselves more and our path becomes so much clearer. We naturally become a role model for others.

This next part of finding myself breaks down the steps I took to creating a happy, healthy and harmonious life.

To living a Sanguine life.

To creating contentment amongst the chaos.

Choosing to thrive in our imperfect world.

Chapter 12
Surrender

"And the day came when the risk to remain tight in a bud was more painful than the risk it took to blossom."

Anaïs Nin

LOST AND FOUND IN THE LAND OF MAÑANA

What exactly does letting go, or surrendering, mean? It doesn't mean that I was giving up or that I was no longer responsible for my actions - quite the contrary. I am definitely still responsible for my actions.

Letting go, for me, means releasing my expectations: surrendering to the Divine and acknowledging that the outcome isn't within my control.

In terms of the things that happen outside of my own body and mind, I have no control. I am not the Mistress of the Universe and honestly, I wouldn't want the job anyway. What I do have power over, however, is how I react to the circumstances that life brings across my path. I can control my actions. Even living, breathing and dying, while I may have certain preferences for such, are not within my control. One day we're here, the next we're not. Without knowing how many days I have in this one precious life, I have to live for this moment, in this moment.

I've had to let go of the need to be right or wrong, to say that something is good or bad. This is not to say that I don't have my opinions about these things, of course, so much as I'd to relinquish the desire to argue or create drama over being Right. What might be good for me is terrible for someone else, and vice versa. Every person's life is different. Every person's life needs to be honored. We each have a Divine light in us. I need to remember to foster that light, stoke it, and let it shine through me, to let people see who I am. I also get the opportunity to take a deep breath and to remember to see the Divine light in everyone else.

Sometimes I'll go outside and just look up. I'll look all around. It doesn't matter if it's a blue sky day or a gray day. If it's night with a new moon, I can still see stars. There is almost always some light. If it's pouring down rain, there's a good chance the night sky will be illuminated by a bolt of lightning. That same light is within me, and you. It is in each of us.

While I may just be a tiny little speck in this gigantic universe, I know that what I'm doing matters. But, since I am just a tiny speck, I have to let go of my expectations and attachments. Every step, every action, everything I do matters. Whether I am here or not, the Earth continues to spin. It will continue beyond us. But that doesn't mean I shouldn't do anything. What I do matters. Every choice I make, every thought I create, word I speak and action I take, matters.

But in practical terms, what does surrender look like? How, specifically, have I let go? When I moved to Costa Rica, I feel like I let go of everything "normal". I had to let go of my physical property when my house was robbed. I had to let go of my expectations for people to show up and be on time and be polite. I had to let go of the idea of how people should show up in the world.

I have had to let go of those things in order to maintain my own inner peace. Sure, I could stamp my feet and demand that it is only professional courtesy to show up on time, but to what end? That is not the culture in which I presently live.

I could keep insisting that things be different and that
I'm Right, but I'd be miserable.

Instead, I choose to keep moving forward. I have to keep putting one foot in front of the other. Rather than exasperating myself trying to rely on others who don't share my worldviews, I instead ask myself to show up in ways that feel integrous and respectful. That's definitely something I enjoy giving to myself. Of course, I want to have a support system - no doubt it's absolutely necessary. But I have to let go of the expectation that they will always be there for me.

It's easier said than done, of course, the whole letting go and surrendering thing. The most essential piece of the puzzle is asking "What no longer serves me in a positive and healthy way?"

With that knowledge, I was armed to create my life with intention, rather than just as a reaction to circumstance or wanting to fit in. Saying no to things, even if I'd previously been all about them, opened new doors and created space in my life for new, fresh things that I wanted to cultivate. Perhaps those doors didn't always open immediately (as the Universe does seem to enjoy testing what I've learned so far) but in hindsight I can see it to have worked perfectly to my benefit each and every time.

There were a few times when I *thought* I had done the work, released expectations, set good boundaries, only to find myself still at an impasse. I found that when I felt like there were a lack of options available, it wasn't because the Universe had given up on me, just that there was more work to be done. I hadn't yet found the right key. When I stilled myself and went within, I was able to understand what was and wasn't working and course correct. Then, and only then, did the new doors show up, as if they had been there all along, just waiting for me to see things from the needed perspective.

Given the number of unfamiliar, uncomfortable and downright unfathomable things in Costa Rica, I had to ask myself the question (as many others had asked me all along): *why do I want to be someplace that isn't working for me?* My answer continues to be that my health is paramount to my familiarity and comfort. I can create any type of life that I want as long as I have my health. So while living in Costa Rica can be difficult, I'm making the most of it. At this point, I am now well acquainted with most of the problems that can arise and through embracing my spiritual path, I can face those trials and tribulations with greater confidence, clarity and authenticity.

I'm not avoiding the problems, running away or hiding out. Ignorance is not bliss. I'm simply choosing to disengage from the drama. I have created my sanctuary within the chaos, my happy place. In this place I am healthy and can create a home that provides me with daily nourishment. Is it my ideal situation? In any given moment the answer is yes. While there may be circumstances outside of my control, I am always growing and allowing life to unfold.

> My ideal life contains the ability to acknowledge that I am happy (AKA sanguine), in this moment and choose not to worry about future moments.

By allowing myself to let go - of my need to be right, to have things my way, on my schedule - ease entered my life. While I still had to put forth effort, it involved far less struggle. By living a life in direct correlation to my values and beliefs, I get to be who I truly am and live a life based on love. In essence, while I still fell down (figuratively, though maybe occasionally literally) I was doing it a lot less.

Surrendering to the present moment brought me more light, love, freedom and openness. Letting go gave me the chance to see myself as a blank slate and opened me up to new opportunities. My potential became limitless.

Basic Necessities: A Shift in Perspective

Before the move, I'd never considered that things like electricity, internet, cable, phone, etc. would be something to take for granted. However, even in a developed country such as Costa Rica, there are still weekly, sometimes daily, challenges with the most basic of things, things that I used to consider an absolute necessity.

To that aim, I've had to let go of the fact that I don't have control over things like doing my laundry, or having water or power on any given day. I've had to adjust to asking questions like "Am I going to have enough propane in the tank to make these muffins in the oven? How long will it be before they replace the propane tank - a few hours, a few days?" Life in the states, with its abundant convenience at every turn, certainly didn't prepare me for such an existence, but I've learned.

I've also had to let go of instant gratification. There is no Amazon, Best Buy, or Target. If my computer breaks, I'm pretty screwed. I'm not so much of a DIY kind of girl and yet I find myself constantly having to do just that. Duct tape and super glue are two of my best friends. For everything. Bowls are held together by duct tape and even my computer has some super glue on it.

I've come to realize that it is my expectation that things be any different that actually causes me to suffer. Sure, I'm used to schedules, 24 hour commerce and reliable utilities but that's not the reality in Costa Rica. When I surrender and release my expectations of how I think things *should* happen, I get to live my life with a bit more ease.

I struggle with my commitment to surrender the most in moments where my unreliable utilities affect my ability to do business. I can't even count the number of times that I've been talking to a client in the U.S. with stable electricity and internet, only to have one or both of mine go out. After fumbling to set up my personal hotspot and returning to the conversation, I usually joke that such things are the hazards of working in the jungle and hope that they can at least empathize if not truly understand. Sometimes they don't.

Another common problem for people who live here is that we have a lot of lightning strikes. When they happen, they can easily fry a hard drive. It hasn't happened to me yet (thank the Universe!), but I've had three electrical cords for the laptop fry already!

I've learned to keep a backup cord, though unfortunately my last one was stolen. For fear that my laptop will eventually die or get fried, I now keep my entire hard drive in Dropbox: all my pictures, videos, documents, and client files. A tourist suggested to me that I should use an external hard drive, fearing that perhaps online cloud systems weren't the most trustworthy. I trust Dropbox more than I trust an external drive that can break (which has happened, losing everything I had on it) or be stolen. Plus my laptop is so old and falling apart (literally) that the USB slot doesn't really work anymore. So I add dropbox into my monthly budget and I'm done.

What's Mine is Yours

Of course, the spotty utilities are less dangerous than the burglaries. I never had any problems when I was traveling but I was always super careful. I stayed in places that had on-site security guards and safes in the rooms. Now that I live here permanently, I have found that burglaries are just commonplace. If you look at community Facebook pages, you'll see a constant stream of people posting: Just got robbed, if you happen to see my (computer, phone, camera, ____, please be in touch).

We have to accept it as a part of our daily lives. This was a total 180 from life in California where, really, the thought of being robbed never entered my mind. Ever.

I've had to surrender to the fact that at some point, I could be robbed again. The place where I live currently isn't secure. The windows in the house have no glass and therefore no locks and they could be broken into. Bars on windows have been broken off, even safes have been pried open.

There is a saying here, something I say all the time: *Así es la vida.* Such is life. I have to accept nothing is permanent and I have to let go of what I think is "mine", what I've earned and what I have worked hard for. I've actually had friends cut out pages in large books and use that as their secret place to store belongings and cash.

Sexism/Racism

Another thing that life in the States led me to take for granted was all of the social justice work that has happened over the past 50-60 years. I know that sexism and racism are still alive and well in the U.S. however, it is rarely as overt as here in Costa Rica.

As a white female, I basically have a double whammy of prejudice working against me. The prevailing notion I've encountered is that unless a woman is your mother, she doesn't deserve your respect.

One of the ways I experienced sexism was in the way that people ignored my instructions, even when they were working for me. I would tell people what I needed them to do and they would just blow me off. (Imagine someone waving their hand at you in "shoo shoo" motion.) Days and weeks would go by and I would not get the work that I needed from them. I would keep asking for it and they would keep telling me they had done it until eventually after sometimes weeks had gone by, they realized that they had indeed screwed up and it was their fault.

I had to resist the urge to say I told you so, if for no other reason that it would have gone unheeded anyway.

Learning to surrender to a culture that views women as less than or unworthy has been unbelievably challenging. It blatantly flies in the face of all that I believe about life, humanity and human dignity. It's not that I don't still believe in equality, but that I have to let go of expecting others to think the same way.

Deep breath. Pause. That's still a hard one for me to swallow.

I still believe that evolution is possible and that an individual can make a difference. Do I think I'm going to change the minds of the 4.7 million people in the country? Probably not, but I might change a few.

Through my example and personal interactions, I might even be able to empower a few women who are so insecure and have so little confidence. So I try to be a role model and help them see that they can stand up for themselves and ask for more from life.

One tiny change - it creates a ripple, one person at a time.

Thanks to my continual shifts in perspective, I've started to look at life in different ways:

When my housekeeper is here and she turns off the fans in order to sweep (or worse, the electricity if off for an undetermined amount of time), it's like a detox. Sweat is dripping off of me but whatever toxins I have in my body are being released.

When a new challenge presents itself, fear is sometimes the first emotion but it's quickly swept away by realism and belief in myself. Whatever the challenge is, I'm not running away. Accepting the things I cannot change, a la The Serenity Prayer, reduces anxiety and worry and it helps shift events into the past.

When I was unsure of where I was going to live, I was faced with vast uncertainty, but at the same time, being in the positive mental space that I was, I overcame that nauseating feeling of *"My god, I have no place to live",* and instead, I asked the question: *"I can live anywhere - where do I want to go?"* Sure, I'd love to have a permanent place in which I can call home, that is spacious and comfortable and mine. But I have to let go of that, it's not happening for me. Not in this moment at least.

My saving grace has been the awareness that there is always a lesson in every experience. I believe in who I am and what I'm doing. My life is in my hands. It's my path.

I had to ask myself: *"What do I want to create? What is something negative that I can let go of? How can I keep moving forward, towards my goal of living a wildhearted life?"*

Negative moments are just that. A moment. I trust my ability to reframe and find the good.

Chapter 13
Acceptance

"Everything can be taken from a man but one thing: the last of the human freedoms—to choose one's attitude in any given set of circumstances, to choose one's own way."

Victor Frankl

So I surrendered: that I don't know what will be. I know what was, and I know what is in this very moment, today. But, I don't know what will be.

Now what?

The next step is acceptance: acceptance of *what is*. Acceptance of who I am, where I am, and what is happening around me. In this very moment, today, I know what is.

The good news? I am not stuck where I am. I can change. I can do anything. I can go anywhere.

So with that unlimited potential (that we each have within ourselves) - because I surrendered – I can now move into acceptance. I accept the beautiful gift that I have become who I am (or, at least, am becoming - slowly but surely).

Acceptance can be a little scary, hence why so many people choose to give up rather than move through the steps. It can be scary to acknowledge who I am. Sometimes I want to step back, not wanting to step into the unknown chapters of my life. But, I know I must continue. I must accept who I am and the gifts I can offer the world. What I can do out in the world is limitless if only, every day, I can practice acceptance of this present moment.

After surrendering to the fact that things are not as I thought they would be when I moved here, after letting go of my expectations, I then moved into acceptance. When I accepted that fact, I had to shift. I had to see my potential, and really my entire life, in a new way.

When I did that, new doors opened for me. I began to see that as much as I wanted to work with clients here, to contribute to this country where I was living, that just wasn't going to happen. Sure, I could get clients - but every client that I worked with treated me in the same abysmal way. While by contrast, every client in other parts of the world treated me with respect and valued what I offered them. I began to realize that Costa Rica was not where I could find quality clients and do the work I love. I needed to be able to find clients in other places with different mindsets, different mentalities.

I also had to accept that there would be barriers for my life in general, barriers that I had no idea existed until I got here. I know it was naïve to think that there wasn't racism and sexism and an overall lack of manners, but that is just so different from who I am, from my upbringing, from the people who I've associated with my entire life. It's difficult to allow – and accept - those kinds of "ism's" into my life and my heart.

I also accepted that as much as I wanted to give to this country where I was living, I had to set boundaries. I had to accept that we (my clients here) would probably never see eye to eye on who I am, my value, and what I can offer. But, at the same time the gift of those experiences were that they allowed me to see my value and my worth more clearly. The more people tried to tear me down, the more strength I found in myself. I accepted that there were people, elsewhere in the world, who did see my light, who did want to work with me, who did value me and who did respect me - all of me.

By surrendering and letting go of the drama, letting go of all the pain and the anger and the sadness that these experiences of feeling devalued had brought into my life, I was able to open up to new ways of living. I was able to create my sanctuary, my happy place, and I was able to accept this new way of life for me - even though it looked nothing like what I had originally thought.

I get to live in a beautiful place with sunshine and summer year round. I get to be greeted by monkeys flying through the trees and cracking open coconuts to drink the water and scoop out the flesh, then dropping them to the ground. I get to live simply and just be present in every moment. Not a day goes by that I'm not grateful. Not a day goes by that I am not in a divine light of acceptance that this is my life - and I love it.

Will it be my life for the next 10, 20, 30 years? That I don't know. I only know that for today I've surrendered and accepted and am fully present in this moment. In fact, in this moment the electricity is out and I'm actually not writing this; I'm using Siri to transcribe what I'm saying. Although he (yes, he) messes up every other word, this is my workaround since my computer is too old and the battery dies so quickly. I accept that the electricity is just going to go off randomly in the middle of the day for no apparent reason, but I can still find ways to do my work. I can still be love. I can still be present in this moment.

I make shifts every time I am confronted with an obstacle. I surrender, and then I accept. I make some changes and I shift the way I think or what I am doing. I'm okay, because I'm doing the work that I love. I have to accept that sometimes the electricity is off, and create a workaround. That may seem like some small little thing, but it is what's happening in this moment and I have to be okay with that - especially since it happens all the time.

I have to take the steps that are necessary to keep moving forward. I can't let myself get stuck in the muddy quicksand. No matter what is thrown at me, I will figure out a way to get through it, and not by cheating or taking shortcuts.

I'm going straight through the muddy river, and I'm going to see it to the other side.

I've had to relinquish my expectation that everyone work like me, think like me and have the same devotion to problem solving that I do. Just because I've learned to create a workaround when the electricity goes out, doesn't mean that everyone else will choose to be as innovative.

I've had the experience of asking a question and receiving such a narrow answer as to be completely unhelpful enough times that I've learned to be very elaborative in this environment. It has been super frustrating for me, but I've also come to accept it as my new normal, and I've had to find ways to work through it in order to get the work done.

Thankfully, as of 2015 I've been blessed with an amazing team. I have been able to find both a Tica and another woman from the States, who share my vision for how to best do the work.

They are on top of their game and submit amazing quality of work without excessive micromanaging from me. My previous experiences with employees that didn't share my commitment to deadlines and quality have made me appreciate them all the more.

Not Giving Up, Except on Unrealistic Expectations

By no means does acceptance mean giving up, but it does mean acknowledging, and getting clear on, *what is*. Of course, *what is* can change. But, acceptance allows me to let go of self-judgment and the constant struggle for perfection which, in turn, helps me grow, both personally and professionally.

Since moving here, I found myself trying to be the perfect someone to everyone – the perfect friend, the perfect vendor to each of my clients, and the perfect boss to my team. Perfection is a burden - and tiring. It can create unrealistic standards that I set not only for myself, but also force onto others. It has also made me feel like nothing I do is ever good enough.

In terms of work, I realized that striving for perfection stripped away my originality and vision because I was so focused on making everything *just right*. This, in turn, ended up consuming the entire creative process and wasted so much time. I kept losing sight of the meaning of things when I was busy making sure my *I's* were dotted and my *T's* were crossed.

By accepting what is, I've gotten so much more clear on what I love to do and what brings me the most joy. And, I've found with this clarity that not only am I being provided with opportunities to work on projects that I love, but I'm also able to choose not to do things that don't serve a positive purpose in my life and business. In the past I would try to do it all, to please everyone. I can't begin to count how many different roles I've tried to play in the last few years of living here, trying to be everything to everyone AND be perfect at it. All the while, more often than not, without getting paid for it.

It took me a while to get to this point and be able to let go of perfection, accepting what is. I am not perfect: ***I am perfectly imperfect.***

Some of the things I've had to accept make perfect sense, even if they are inconvenient, like animals having their very own wake up/noise schedule. Others seem odd and quirky to me, though I have to invite them in as well.

For example, one of my past housekeepers was contracted to come Tuesday and Friday, yet she still always asked at the beginning of each week if I wanted her to come. I was raised to take contractual obligations very seriously, but that isn't a cultural norm here. I was also raised in a culture that valued customer service and going the extra mile. While it's true that there are many employees in the States that don't adhere to this philosophy, it is still highly valued and praised. In Costa Rica, like I mentioned, I can go into the vet's office or the hardware store or a supermarket and they will tell me "mañana" or "in 15 days" or "let me take down your number and I'll call you when I find out". But, experience has taught me that they will rarely (if ever) actually take the steps to find out. And they definitely don't call. It's only making additional visits, being right there in front of them, that they will eventually do what you're asking of them.

As crazy making as the culture shock can be at times, I recognize that I have to set the standards for how to keep my own commitments and not get so wrapped up in how others keep theirs. True, in terms of my business, I need to find employees who have the same work philosophy to keep workflow going. In the rest of my life though, I get to adjust to a different pace, even if it isn't one I would have dictated.

Is my spirit broken? No. That would mean that I would be accepting suffering. Rather, I accept the pain - that is real. But I know there's no reason to suffer through it. I know that I engage in far more suffering when I keep letting the thoughts of how "wrong" it is to do things another way run rampant. That makes the suffering increase exponentially because then it's not just the conversation with someone who doesn't intend to follow through but the addition of all the time I obsess over it. I choose to minimize my suffering, so I shift and make changes instead.

Making Do

I make adjustments all the time. I can't go to the store and expect to have a plethora of options available to me. In the last few years I'll say that the selection is definitely improving: the options are increasing, but there's always that day when I want **X**, and it's nowhere to be found. But that's just what I *want*. I then have to accept that maybe what I *want* isn't really what I *need*. Maybe I don't need 20 options of facial soap. Can I find contentment with just the one?

I have learned an amazing amount of workarounds for culinary creations. I've learned how to make homemade vegan peanut butter and chocolate ice cream. I've learned how to make raw dehydrated gluten free bread. Gluten free pizza with cashew cheese and an abundance of rich toppings. Frozen lime coconut tarts. Hungry yet?

Without all the clothing options of the States, I make do by enlisting my housekeeper who sews the holes in my current clothes. As I mentioned, my 18 year-old sheets are so old they tear just by looking at them. Overall, I've learned to live with a whole lot less. I've learned to live with everything being old and falling apart without having the option to run out to the store and buy something new and shiny.

Some of my friends here think I still have more than I need, but in reality if I were in the States, my life, my wardrobe, my bedding, and my kitchen would look a whole lot different. I've learned that here, this is all I need. I wouldn't go so far as to say I want for nothing - but I do want for a whole lot less.

And you know those moments when the electricity goes out? I've learned to embrace these moments, to find a little bit of peace and to return to the present moment. I grab one of my books (like a real book with actual paper pages) and sit on the terrace and read, or even just sit on the terrace and do nothing. It's okay to do nothing sometimes. And that lesson right there is one of the true gifts of acceptance! I certainly wasn't embracing downtime while I was running around with perfection infection.

While in the U.S. I could get almost anything I wanted at any time of year, I've learned to embrace that certain foods are only available at certain times: the crazy looking mamon chinos, water apples, mangoes falling off the trees, and even cashews. By embracing the seasonal nature of these items, I get to be giddy with expectation when I go to the farmer's market or see a guy on the corner with a truck bed full of mamon chinos, with their funny soft spikes sticking out of them. There is something to be said for delayed gratification.

Mindful Acceptance

I make it a habit to notice what my thoughts are focused on. Where do my thoughts go during the day? What words do I use, and are they positive or negative, helpful or harming? I write down my journey and review it continuously. What is my *why*? Why am I here? I set an intention for each day and for each part of the journey.

Setbacks are also a part of the journey. When we're open to it, they create more awareness rather than dragging us down into the land of stuck. They allow us a do-over so that we may start again, with fresh ideas.

Question – what have I learned so far? What more do I know I need to learn (knowing that sometimes, the lesson will appear without realizing that I needed it)?

Answer – Living in the moment. I have to show up, with what I have available to me, and do the work. Internet goes out? I turn on my personal hotspot. Water gets turned off? I have a spare bottle in the fridge. That's super important for mornings when there's no water and coffee must be made. Because... priorities.

I am continuously learning the art of patience. Life really does move at a sloth's pace here. Like I've said again and again, mañana does not mean "tomorrow" here. Either I

have to accept that, or I have to find a workaround.

I have had to learn how to go with the flow and be in the moment. My living situation in this moment is not ideal, but I make the most of it.

I recognize that I can change it, eventually, and I begin to plant seeds to help me along the way. I acknowledge the things that are good about where I'm living, so that I remain in a more positive and content state. This helps improve my overall outlook on life and creates a sense of ease in the more difficult moments.

I move forward, fueled by internal strength. I make every attempt to accept and understand the value of my failures and live a more whole life through creating a ever constant happy, healthy and harmonious outlook.

Chapter 14

Self-Growth

"In all realms of life it takes courage to stretch your limits, express your power, and fulfill your potential."

Suze Orman

About 9 months into living here, I started to sense that my life would be changing. I knew my cat Harmony was coming to the end of his life and I would no longer have his presence with me. I looked back at all I had done – moving to Costa Rica, writing books, starting my own business, getting my yoga certification, going to graduate school, and getting my health coaching certification. I thought to myself: I've done everything I've wanted to do in life. Sure, there were shifts and changes, but my life felt whole. I was only 38 at the time and knew my life was not yet complete.

I had free time. I had money in the bank. I was able to work with amazing people and give back to others with time, money and opportunities. Life was good. Life was exactly what I'd always wanted it to be.

> But when you've accomplished everything on your to-do list, the question becomes: *Now what?*

It was time for me to grow. I had surrendered, and I had accepted. It was time to evolve into something new, different and maybe even better, become truer to myself in the process. I had a choice: I could plant the seeds, nurture them and allow them to grow into truly beautiful flowers, or I could do "just enough" to maintain. In my mind, maintaining is stagnant and that would be pretty much the equivalent to letting my flowers wither and die.

Self-growth requires valuing both the good and the bad. All the struggles, difficulties, and challenges: those gave me the fuel to keep moving forward. I could have thrown myself into neutral, or retreated, but I knew that the best thing to do was to see these difficulties as energy boosters, and to keep pushing forward.

> I asked myself:
> What motivates me?
> What new experiences do I want to create?

I believe that new experiences allow us to live more fully, to step into new levels of consciousness. They help us push ourselves further and to blossom fully into our truly beautiful selves.

Looking within, while difficult at times, allows me to go beyond what I could possibly imagine in my life. Too many times in my life I have thought that the answers laid somewhere outside of me, while the reality is that by connecting to the truth of my being and Divinity *within*, the possibilities are endless. I know that by nurturing my spirit, I can do anything I want. My gender doesn't matter, nor my race, or even how much money is in my bank account. I can do anything I desire; I only have to put my heart into it.

Having been so lost and working my way back into my inherent harmony, I had to look deeply inside who I was and how I was showing up in the world - and how I *wanted* to show up in the world. I had to make the connection between my heart and my mind. Often times those were conflicted: like my heart telling me to take on another Costa Rica client (because the referral came from a friend) even though my mind said *"Don't do it!!!"*.

What I needed was to get to a place where my heart and my mind were no longer in conflict, where my body, mind, heart, and soul - the divine within me - were all equal. It was a huge undertaking. There was no magic wand that I could wave and make everything line up exactly as I wanted. But, by doing some intensive self-actualization work, I managed to come face to face with my unlimited potential.

Connecting everything together, I remembered the beauty within and all of the gifts that I wanted to share with the world. I allowed myself to be seen and heard: first by myself, my own inner knowing, and then by others.

The path to self-discovery and awareness certainly wasn't quick. Of course, I'm still on it, but I know that it took me a while to get to a place where I feel like I understand who I am and what I want to give, how I want to show up in the world and serve.

I had to ask myself big questions and do the work to understand what the answers meant, deep down in the fiber of my being:

Who am I?
What do I want to give?

How I want to show up in the world? How do I want to serve?

I want to show up in the world as a divine light. As someone who is nurturing and caring, giving and extending lovingkindness to all. I want to share my gifts with the world. I truly believe that inside of me I have this gift to give...I think we all have gifts and talents, and I want to be able to share mine with the world. This is all fine and well until I run into someone - or multiple someone's- who don't appreciate my gifts. The temptation in those moments is to let their opinion diminish how I feel about what I have to offer.

I've had to accept that not everyone is going to be nice nor are they always going to understand who I am and my way of life. As I continue to grow and become who I am, looking within, I know that I am a good person. I am not perfect, but I am a generous, loving and kind person. So while I may not always understand why everyone is not going to be nice to me (as that is their prerogative), I still need to do my own inner work and show up. I still need to extend love out into the world. Everything I do stems from love.

Of course, while it can be challenging to accept people who don't value what I have to offer, the bigger problem is when I let others' opinions cause me to doubt myself. It's a simple fact of life that not everyone will like me or value what I have to share. However, those opinions mean very little. My responsibility isn't to those who don't get me but rather to Spirit and myself. I have to honor my own calling and learn to tune out the feedback of those who have no interest in seeing me thrive as my best version of myself.

I know that I have to keep showing up and eventually I'll find the people who will listen and who believe in me and will want to be a part of my community of open-minded souls.

I've always been resilient, but that resiliency has been tested here. Personal growth requires learning how to minimize suffering and find healthy perspectives when life gets a little rough. I've had people intentionally set me up to fail - and yet I still come out ahead.

My personal growth went something like this:

First, I was honest with myself. I accepted that I was not perfect and that I didn't need to be (trust me, easier said than done).

Life is constantly giving me twists and turns, and the only way to grow is to understand that sometimes, I'll make mistakes. I also stopped comparing myself to others. I did the work. I got help along the way, but it was my responsibility to show up and do the work in front of me as if it was for Spirit itself, because I believe that all work really is unto Spirit, no matter how small the task.

I realized that I was responsible for my own happiness. No person, situation or place could make me happy. I had to find it within myself first.

I am continuously letting go of that which does not serve me. Moving on from the past. Learning the lessons and living in the present.

I believe in myself.

CHRISSY GRUNINGER

I remember that, even in the darkest of times, there is always light to be found.

I return to the present moment when life gets a little muddled. I return to my breath. I remember that I make my own happiness. I actively pursue my goals. Every day, I do a little something to make my dreams happen, even if it's just taking a moment to remind myself of what they are.

I do more than *just good enough*... there is always more that I can do. Not in a perfectionist way but in a way of always growing and expanding.

I laugh at myself. The small things really are just small things. I stress less and I remember to look at the big picture.

While my inherent harmony was already within, I needed to continuously examine and bring it forward, into the light to allow it to illuminate my path. By growing I get to connect even more deeply to the oneness that exists in each of us and our world. I get to be more open, vulnerable and free from any shadows that might try to take me off course.

I live every day outside of my comfort zone and, therefore, I am always growing. I realize that even with all the pain and the perplexing moments, inside of me is more confidence than I had originally thought. I just have to be willing to see it and honor it.

As I developed my confidence, my authenticity,

my daily presence, I was able to grow into a fuller expression of myself. This presented its own challenges, as not everyone understood the difference between confidence and arrogance.

I have had to find the balance between being confident, stepping into the role of knowing exactly who I am and what I can offer, and being seen as arrogant by people who are insecure and unsure of what they bring to the table. And sometimes, the perceived arrogance was due to some peoples' beliefs that I shouldn't be so confident and authoritative as a woman. In a culture where women are often instructed to be seen and not heard, my owning my own power and skill wasn't always an easy sell.

For example, I was once told that because I'm a woman, I needed to be seen with the owner of a company (a man) in order to gain the respect of his staff (all men). It wasn't that they needed to respect me for who I was on my own, or to listen to what I had to say (to be "heard"). I only needed to "be seen".

There were people who tried to bring me down during this time of self-reflection, and I had a choice: I could find the strength within to either not give them my attention and continue to move forward on my path, or I could listen and remain stuck.

Some people approach life from a perspective of survival. In my own experience, I'd way rather do the work of surrendering, accepting, and continuing to move forward, rather than settle for the best I can see at the time. Granted, those on different spiritual paths may not see an option beyond survival mode. I struggle not to think of my way as Better, as opposed to just better for me personally. It can be hard to watch others refuse freedom, but I let that strengthen my resolve to find ways to pursue it whenever possible. I'm going to carpe the heck out of this diem and live intensely, with intention.

This is when life gets real. And fulfilling. And intense.

> As soon as I stopped surviving, reacting, reaching — I started thriving, responding, and holding steady within the abundant space that exists within me.

There were tears — of happiness, sadness, and anger — and there were smiles, and belly laughs, and feelings of weightlessness. My inner fire burns so brightly now that people often wonder what new regimen I've embraced. That new regimen is the choice of a life well lived: wildhearted, meaningful, fulfilling LIFE.

I'm continuously evolving on the path of my life. And when I say "evolve", that's the nice way of saying that I've had to face some really hard life lessons. What's kept me continuing forward is not only my resilience, but my ability to dig deep and find the drive inside of myself to continuously take that next step. To never give up.

I've taken a lot of deep breaths. I've taken a lot of time on my own to regroup and remember who I am and why I'm here. I've re-evaluated who I am and made sure I'm still on the right path. I've asked myself some hard questions.

In order to decide where I wanted to go with my life, I took stock of where I had been. I journaled quite a lot about the experiences since childhood that had shaped my character. Looking back, I could see the path I'd taken and how every choice I've made had placed me squarely at that place of reflection.

I grew up in an affluent area of Los Angeles and while other parents were spoiling their children beyond their wildest dreams, my parents insisted that I work for the luxuries my peers took for granted. I started working at a preschool, getting paid under the table because I wasn't technically old enough to have a job. (Shhh, don't tell the IRS or child labor for that matter). At 14, I had my first official job, working in a frozen yogurt shop, serving my classmates as they came in to spend their parents' money.

The disparity between my inherited work ethic and the frivolous pursuits of my classmates led me to ask my parents to find some way for me to go to the high school off "the hill" and be with the other "normal" kids, a request that went un-granted.

As I got through college and into my 20's, I would often lie about where I came from. I didn't want people making assumptions about me based on a lifestyle I'd desperately wanted to enjoy but never had.

Looking back, I can see why my parents wanted us to grow up with an independent mindset, although now I find it amusing that they wonder where I got the notion to be independent enough to become an expatriate.

It might not be my kindest and most loving thought, but I sometimes think that if they'd wanted me to get a high paying job in the States, with a husband, 2 kids, a white picket fence and a golden retriever, then perhaps they should have spoiled me like the other kids were in my neighborhood. As that's what a lot of them did.

And I could have had that – I could have married my college boyfriend, had a few kids and then... eventually... gotten divorced. I wouldn't have been happy in that life, but my hard working 14-year-old self didn't know that and sometimes the old resentments resurface until I look at them head on and see how much better off I am.

I wasn't any less confused in my 20s. After I got out of a long, drawn out, bad relationship in the first half of my 20's, I spent the next 5 years attempting to find myself in what everyone around me considered normal.

My friends and I would meet up for happy hour after our work days had finished; we'd have a few half priced drinks and split some appetizers, maybe followed up by dinner and good conversation. We'd talk about our lives, jobs, politics, world events, art, and music. We took weekend trips around California, got on-the-glass seats at hockey games and 3rd baseline seats at baseball games. We had full time jobs, bought homes, drove nice cars and went to live concerts and festivals. It was the average life of an upper middle class 20 something and it didn't even occur to me to look for other options.

My desire to keep up with the Joneses was just the result of some leftover insecurities from my teen years - something I thankfully grew out of.

In hindsight, I can see how these experiences led up to my decision to seek something different, something more. I can even see how things overlap and repeat themselves. When I was 14 and had that job at the frozen yogurt shop, I was made a supervisor within just a few months. I was supervising people who were several years older than me, and it usually didn't go over well that a 14 year old kid was telling them what to restock or deciding whether or not they could have a day off. The manager saw my leadership potential because I showed up with competence and confidence, not unlike the way I still approach my work in Costa Rica, even when it's equally unappreciated.

When I didn't get married at 25, that opened up a whole new world of possibilities.

I bought a house, went back to graduate school and started traveling more. I started writing because it was something that, deep down, I truly enjoyed. I got certified in yoga and health coaching, two things that I love and are deeply a part of who I am. And one of the places that I happened to travel to was Costa Rica, which is where I met Troy, which brought me to write a book about my travels, which got me a job working here, which eventually helped me move here.

None of that would have been possible if I didn't have the courage within to grow, if I didn't know who I was and how I wanted to show up in the world. Finding my path became even more clear.

I always knew that certain actions I had taken in the past had led me to where I am now, but I had never really seen it written down. When I did, everything made perfect sense.

My path to living and working here wasn't straight or easy. If you've read my other books, you remember the potholes and speed bumps in the road (literally and figuratively) that were trying to prevent me from moving forward.

All of the puzzle pieces eventually fit together, but that isn't because I had some magic formula or wand. It was through trial, and a whole lot of error, that I made them fit and continue to make them fit. I have a vision for my life, and while that can change when new circumstances present themselves, the underlying value does not.

All I can do is continue to do the work and show up as my best self. Part of letting go of perfectionism is gaining the freedom that comes with the knowledge that it's ok to have a bad day! I catch myself when I say things like "I'm having a bad day." Instead of focusing on it, I say something to reinforce the positive: "Things are not going well today. And I'm going to do *xyz* to turn it around." I focus on what I can do rather than staying stuck in the negativity.

Little by little, those steps become daily routines and the bigger picture becomes more clear and do-able. Life isn't so overwhelming when

I break it down and begin with a single step.

When I focus inward, I develop a stronger sense of myself and my capacity. I'm not always looking for the next big thing. Being so in tune with my inherent harmony, I know I can be a positive influence in the world. Becoming self-aware allows me to see both my positive qualities and my areas of opportunity for improvement.

I become more aware of how I'm showing up in the world, and I can make adjustments to my daily actions. By continuously taking a self-assessment, by showing up, doing the work and staying motivated, I develop more inner strength, awareness and confidence - which in turn gives me more courage, strength and presence.

Negativity breeds negativity

I know that when I'm in a space of efficiency and organization, a greater percentage of positive outcomes occur. Much more work gets done. Growth becomes more than just expansive, but fun.

For me, negativity isn't just an attitude. It's a basic lack of integrity: stealing, cheating, under-delivering on promises, lying about one's capabilities, or being inefficient. It's deadlines and responsibilities being put on hold because of someone not doing what they said they would do. It's gossiping about others or spreading rumors. That is all in the negativity box, and that box has been thrown into the compost.

During this time of growth, I got organized. For

a time I had a feeling of being disheveled in my personal and professional life, which was dismantling my intentions and blocking me on the path I was trying to follow.

I also had to build up my resilience. I had to adopt new ways to envision my most wildhearted life.

> I stepped back and took a look at the big picture: What was going right?

I recognized that what was happening in the moment wouldn't necessarily be the same in the future. I chose to change the path and direct my energy, focusing on more positive and productive outcomes.

I am always creating the bright side. Every dark moment has one. Often times it's a lesson to be learned so that we don't have to repeat this moment again. I say "create" because it is much more intentional than just looking for it or asking someone else to hand it to me. Sometimes it requires a little more internal fortitude but the alternative is swimming around in a disempowered state, wishing I could control things that aren't even mine to work on.

One step at a time

I had to figure out where I was and what I needed, in the moment. Did I need support? Did I need to take a walk and get some fresh air? Did I need to prepare a healthy meal that would nourish my body, heart, mind and spirit?

I know I can't always plan for everything, but taking care of myself and developing my ability to be resilient allows me to adjust and shift in order to continue moving forward. Flexibility is a key to growth and resiliency. When life doesn't go as planned or roadblocks show up and try to derail me, I've got excellent pivot muscles.

When I'm struggling, on a day when life makes my heart race, body shake or leaves me pacing back and forth in my little house, I pause, close my eyes, and put my hands over my heart center. I take a few deep breaths. With every breath, I feel my body relax a little more. I feel the pain sensations in my body dissipate. I sense my inherent harmony and begin to feel whole again.

The truth is that no matter what someone says or does, that only affects the surface, maybe bruises my ego, but it doesn't even come close to touching the divinity within. If I can get back in touch with the truth of my being, I'm golden.

If that doesn't work, (not due to it being ineffective but rather sometimes I'm just not ready to shift my feelings of blame, guilt and shame) I then make a "to feel" list.

In times of uncertainty, I know I must become more aware of the discomfort and acknowledge what is happening.

I ask my authentic self:

How am I feeling physically?
How am I feeling emotionally?
How am I feeling mentally?
How am I feeling spiritually?

There are moments when I still feel empty, lonely, depressed, disappointed, discouraged, frustrated, sad, angry, and overwhelmed. Yet I have to shift that energy; I can't stay stuck. What I'll often do is make a list of all that I do have and how that makes me feel. I notice where I am settling and I ask how can I push myself a little further.

Once I get a clearer picture of the problem, then I can take action and either let go, or redirect the energy into something else. I go from being my hard self to my soft self. I linger in the moments of being happy, satisfied, and fulfilled.

I ask myself about the lessons I can learn from the more challenging moments in life. I know that I can learn from my mistakes, my missteps, when I really examine them. Sometimes the best I could do in a past moment due to stress or external factors, pales compared to what I'm capable of when I'm grounded and centered. I reframe and get back to work acknowledging that my improved state of mind/body/spirit will lead to a more positive outcome.

I know that avoiding and repressing my feelings will keep me feeling them over and over again. That nauseous feeling? It's not going away until I resolve the issue. So, I feel it but I give it an expiration date. Dwelling in the negative, telling the same story of wrong to anyone who will listen can be alluring but it doesn't serve me. I can't run away from my problems, no matter how many people validate that they are real or shouldn't be happening.

I celebrate the small victories in life. Sometimes, when I'm down on myself or others, it's a result of only focusing on what hasn't happened according to plan. When I pause to honor what is going well, I can create more of that. Gratitude goes a long way in creating additional things to be grateful for, just as negativity breeds more things to be disappointed in.

Another major piece of spiritual growth is pushing myself out of my comfort zone. In my comfort zone, I only live up to what I already know I'm capable of and miss all sorts of opportunities. I'd say that right about the time I moved to Costa Rica, I gave up almost all semblance of a comfort zone and wow, did my growth sky rocket as a result. It can be painful occasionally, but it's that pain that has motivated me to get to know and rely on my authentic self.

Fear, if I give it the opportunity, keeps me in my comfort zone. It prevents me from growing. If I can work through the fear and do what I set out to do, I realize it was just a mental state and not an actual physical deterrent.

What I often tell myself is that if I make a mistake or fall off the path, I don't have to worry. I can start over and return to the present. I can let go of the past and accept that it happened. Then I take a deep breath, and grow from the experience.

I cultivate patience, knowing not everything has to happen right now, in this instant.

I give myself space to breathe, change and grow.

I make my life happen. I believe in myself.

I have to live my truth, even if it's not always well received.

I have to fall in love - with myself, then with the world around me. I look beyond what I have and into *who I am.*

Every time something ends in my life, it is a chance to grow and start fresh, to begin again. I only have to be open to receiving the new and trust the process.

Chapter 15
Self-Care

"Women need real moments of solitude and self-reflection to balance out how much of ourselves we give away."

Barbara de Angelis

This country truly beat me down. My friend who had lived here for over a decade told me it would do so, reassuring me that it wasn't just me. Nonetheless, it was still a challenge sometimes to get through the day.

There were days when I truly felt like someone was banging on the top my head with a mallet and hammering me into the ground. I could see myself as this once-whole being reduced to a pile of broken bones. Funny in Saturday morning cartoons - not so funny in real life.

I was overwhelmed, exhausted, and in a constant state of anxiety from the break-ins. I was also so tired of having to fight with people to prove that I am as intelligent and worthy of respect even if I'm not a man or Costa Rican.

So not what I pictured as my life on the Rich Coast.

I remember a beautiful thing that a friend once said to me: *Sometimes we choose an environment that beats us down to break us and bring out the most brilliant ray of light that we carry.*

That was exactly how I felt. Recognizing my inherent harmony was that brilliant ray of light, and finding my happy place amongst the destruction was how I was going to be able to get through the day. More so, it was how I was going to share all the beauty that I've found in living a wildhearted life.

I'm honestly at a point in my life where I don't need much. I don't need to go out and party, and I don't want to actually. That would be the opposite of caring for myself. Waking up and feeling hungover is not my idea of a good time. I want to be putting as much positive energy into my body and spirit and heart and life as possible. For me, alcohol only diminishes that, and drives me down.

For all those struggling with an addiction to drugs or alcohol, I believe that their dependence upon those stimuli are their own best ideas about self-care, with the consciousness that they have now. It's not really *care*, as it's essentially poisoning the body, but it does absolutely achieve the goal of putting a temporary buffer between a person and their problems.

I don't understand it or choose it for myself.

I do my best not to judge it, though it's never been my path, because I see it as their form of reprieve from whatever demons they are facing. I'm guessing that a similar line of thought could be applied for all of the infidelity I see around me. Perhaps makes them feel more powerful, or carefree or helps them to escape their reality for a moment.

We all have things that we do to get through the day and a buffet of options to distract us from our truth. While some of us could never imagine binge drinking our problems into oblivion, we could absolutely try to shop them away or eat them away or even entertain them away. There's a reason that Netflix has so many subscriptions. Who has time for problems while cramming in 100 and something episodes of Bones or Gilmore Girls?

I do my best to seek out healthy and positive outlets, as well as sacred space, which allows me to be in a more positive place and do more out in the world. What I've found is that, in Costa Rica, my self-care practices look different than when I was living in California. Here, without a car and money, I find self-care in the most simple of moments. It could be sleeping in or playing with my kittens and watching them chase a gecko (or, god forbid, a gigantic cockroach). My home is my sanctuary, and I consider being in my home a form of self-care. It is where I feel safe and comfortable.

Other forms of self-care I practice:

There are times when I walk around the little town of Quepos, without any real purpose or intention, just to see what is new and good.

I love going to the farmers market on Saturdays. I usually don't buy much, but I love to interact with the farmers and see all the beautiful varieties of color and texture. Plus, it's on the malecón, so it's a lovely place to simply be and watch the rolling tides.

I might walk down to the beach and feel the sand beneath my feet as the warm water washes up over them. I can sense the sunshine radiating down on my skin as a cold, albeit overpriced, cocktail is brought to my lounge chair.

Then there's my daily yoga practice, both on and off the mat. When I prepare healthy food, or enjoy the sunrise breaking through my curtains, or watch the sunset as it casts a golden hue on the mango trees outside my kitchen window - I know these simple moments to be my version of self-care.

Ultimately, I want to live a quiet life. These are a few self-care practices that help me to do just that. But, that's not enough.

Self-care also includes not taking on too much. I set boundaries and only accept commitments that truly feel right in my heart. I have learned how to say no... for the most part.

I work on my goals. Whether it's learning Spanish, writing this book or working on maintaining my health, there is always something I can be doing to expand my consciousness and ability to be of service and live an authentic life.

I only put my attention where I truly feel like it will be of benefit to myself and/or others.

I meditate and get on the mat. Sometimes my meditation is taking a walk out in nature, or spending time photographing the early morning birds.

I re-read sections out of my favorite books.

I take naps.

I prepare really yummy meals; not always super healthy, but always delicious.

I talk with my cats. It's true: I am a crazy cat lady. However, I only ever say good things. I don't want to bring down their energy and, by staying positive, I lift up my own energy.

I maintain a clean, inspired, fresh home. I leave the shoes at the door, and I do the dishes every night before bed. I also have my housekeeper come twice per week.

Day to day living

A day in the life of good self-care might look like the following:

Waking up naturally between 5 and 6 a.m.

Immediately opening the curtains, allowing the sunrise to filter through and the fresh morning air to come inside.

Dry brushing

Drinking warm water with lime

Yoga or walking to the beach

Showering

Drinking a smoothie, then coffee

No using the phone or computer after 5 p.m.

Eating dinner by 6

Tidying up

Practicing a bit of yoga

Watching a show/movie

Reflecting on the successes of the day, and letting go of the negatives

Sleeping by 9

All of these practices promote good physical (body), mental (mind/clarity), emotional (heart), and spiritual (soul) self-care.

Experiencing it all

I also allow myself to feel sad, angry, and bewildered. Feeling these emotions, and allowing myself to go deeply into them, helps me to not only acknowledge that they exist, but to also take action to overcome them. This helps me to appreciate the beautiful moments even more.

Other than happiness, emotions do not seem to be well-accepted here - especially anger. Matthew Hutson wrote in an article for Psychology Today:

"Anger does not merely benefit the individual. It also fuels social progress. It stimulated the civil rights and gender equality movements. It can bring about fairness, justice, boldness, and clarity. Without it the downtrodden might never be heard. If you always muzzle your frustration when your partner does something you don't like, your problem may never come to light, which can corrode the relationship from within."

My experience of Costa Rica brings me to the following two points: there seems to be very little innovation here and a great deal of inequality. Innovation and social progress seem to lag behind the United States. Men and women do not appear to share their feelings and their relationships suffer.

Intelligent conversations are also a brilliant part of my self-care. I haven't made a lot of friends here in Manuel Antonio because of my experience in Tamarindo. I accepted that it was necessary for me to be more on my own, because in any Costa Rica beach or ex-pat community there are going to be problems.

There are going to be people who don't like each other, who act like they're the cool crowd, the Big Man on Campus, and who gossip and demean others, and that, again, diminishes my light. Just like alcohol, it's not something that I need. There are a few people here who I think are real. And to the surprise of some, I have both Tico and ex-pat friends.

I'll also instant message or Skype with friends. I've got friends all around the world, and I love comparing and contrasting our lives. While these people are far away, they're still a very big part of my life, and I am grateful for them. I remember one night when a newly made friend was visiting and I hung out with him at the hotel pool until 3 a.m., just talking and laughing over a nice bottle of red wine.

> Talking with another person about real life, actual intelligent conversation, is like an instant energetic refresher in my body, mind and spirit. I leave good conversations recharged, ready to face whatever may be headed my way.

Self-care is also acknowledging the little gifts from the universe. One day a friend contacted me and I was honest about my "retreat" style of living - and she told me she does the same. She knew so many others who were also withdrawing from the chaos to lead a simpler, quieter life.

Then there was the day that I so needed a hug. I was being judged for my strange lifestyle and for not being a "nice person" - and I was feeling really down. And then a message appeared from Tico friend, sending me an *abrazo*. While technically hugs are care from others, building and caring for the relationships with people who might give them to me is absolutely part of how I take care of myself.

Self-care is being in service to myself when I say no to that which does not serve me or my purpose. I am in disservice when I say Yes to something I know I should've refused. I do not want to have to honor my commitment and trudge through a pile of mud while I'm doing so.

Living my values is self-care. Showing up in the world as who I truly am allows me to do more in an authentic, wild-hearted way.

I can go so much farther in my daily life if I practice self-care throughout the day.

When I wake up, I ground myself by taking 3 deep, mindful breaths. This allows me time to transition from sleeping, to the day, while staying in the present moment. I have stopped checking my phone the moment I wake up, a terrible habit I got myself into for a while.

I actually read a blog once where a woman had quit all social media (but I suppose her blog was not social media in her eyes). She said Satan had taken over social media and by being on social media, she was not being in God's presence. I think that might be pushing things a bit too far but by giving myself this quiet, non-digitized space in the morning, I am much more ready to begin the day when I do finally sit down at my computer.

I make a list of what absolutely needs to get done that day. If I happen to get everything done by 10 a.m., then I can choose to either take the day off or look ahead and see what's coming up and decide if I want to start on the next round of projects.

I'm not a big fan of wasting time. I believe time is precious and valuable. In recognition of these facts, I know that boundary setting is also a crucial part of my self-care. Sometimes, the only way to get out of the situation is to leave. Quit the job. End the friendship... I must take care of me. Toxic relationships, be it personal or professional, will only make me more stressed and overwhelmed.

As a business owner, there is often an expectation from clients that I be available to them 24/7. In the beginning, I did my best to accommodate that notion. After all, I was raised in the land of "The Customer is Always Right". Not only is making myself available at any hour unsustainable but also unprofessional. Businesses typically have hours of operation. If I allow clients to dictate my schedule, rather than communicating when I'm available, I'm being a terrible boss, of myself.

Once I remembered my right to create my business in a way that allowed me to have a life, I felt freer (and liked my business more!). I also communicate with my clients more, like for example, if I need more time. Previously, I would have tried to white knuckle it and get the job done, even if I was tired or faced with impossible timelines. These days, I'm much more direct about what needs I have to complete a project and I find that my clients respect me more because I'm being open and honest. I'm not lying, hiding, setting unrealistic expectations that I know I can't keep and that keeps the overall quality of my work high.

Sometimes, it's difficult being an entrepreneur. We don't get paid vacation days or holiday bonuses and sometimes making sure that my employees get compensated for their time adequately means that I get paid what's left, as opposed to compensating adequately for my own time. The buck stops here. I am constantly having to accept ownership of everything.

Something that I am happy to do, especially when it comes to protecting my team, but it's also very wearing. Yet another reason to have excellent self-care practices in place.

What I've learned is that many opportunities will present themselves to me but I don't necessarily need to take them all. Prioritizing not only my tasks and the tasks of my team but also who and what is most important to focus on in order to continue my business and sustain its growth and well-being, is key. Providing my team with priorities is, in and of itself, self-care as I don't have to worry that things won't get done or that the most important things will slip through the cracks.

I learned to slow down, take breaks and take more time to do nothing, embracing the quiet. Allowing myself downtime also provides new opportunities for inspiration to strike. When I'm constantly in a state of go-go-go, I often can't hear the signals that others (or the universe) are sending me. Being in a quiet state gives me more presence and enables me to listen rather than always be the source of output.

Ways I recharge

Even though I mentioned Netflix as a potential addictive behavior, I have actually found that binge watching a few hours (as opposed to All Day or a few days) allows me time to relax and recharge my mind. Especially if it's a show that I've already seen as I'm not having to think about character development or remembering what happened last week. It's a way that I give my brain a break and recharge for the days ahead.

As with alcohol, for me, it's about moderation. I'm all for an umbrella drink on the beach now and then or a tv episode or 2, I just don't want either to become the focus of my life. I have way too much I want to do for either of those things to take on leading roles in my life.

Similarly, spending time alone is like hitting the refresh key. I'm able to create more clarity during moments of quiet insight than if I'm always surrounded by external noise and other people's comings and goings.

I sometimes also do a total 180 from my regular life and take a digital detox.

Generally, people who practice self-care on a regular basis are happier and more productive. I know that's something I want more of!

As a part of both self-growth and self-care, I take risks – I will never know the happiness that may be just around the corner if I never try.

Regarding relationships, I am super clear on what types of relationships I want in my life. I want mature, uplifting, drama-free relationships where people value who I am (and vice versa) – both in my personal life as well as my professional. I still miss the red flags at times but I will often get out of the situation a whole lot faster...creating more peace and presence in my life than if it had dragged out.

I stop complaining. I don't mean to say that I'm pushing all my feelings down. What I mean is – I get out of the situation that is causing me so much turmoil. Either I find a way to fix it, accept it or leave.

I am kind to myself – negative self-talk gets me nowhere. I show up every day with a fresh new me. I put aside any bad habits of yesterday and start again. I have stopped saying "I should" and decide to either do it or let it go or find a way around.

While I don't allow negative self-talk I also do not allow others opinions of me to affect my own self-worth. I have learned that not everyone will like me. Not everyone will understand me. When I internalize external forces and negativity, I let go of my own control over the situation and give someone else the power. That's *no bueno*.

And most importantly...

I ask myself: what sustains me? What brings me joy, light, harmony, excitement, wonder?

Chapter 16

Gratitude

*"Cultivate the habit of being grateful for every good thing that comes to you, and to give thanks continuously.
And because all things have contributed to your advancement, you should include all things in your gratitude."*

Ralph Waldo Emerson

Gratitude.

Big topic these days.

It seems like everyone's got a gratitude list or a daily practice. Hundreds of books on the topic, 84,000,000 results on Google. Why gratitude?

Because sometimes life seems to flow altogether too fast, we forget to stop along the way and smell the roses. We lose track of those simple moments in life that create lightness - or create light when it feels like there is only darkness.

For me, gratitude brings light to the dark moments in my life.

While I believe in always trying to see the "big picture", I also believe that, often times, we overlook the smaller things in life.

So how do I seek out the smaller things?

I get outdoors and enjoy the vast landscapes - and the little things I find along the way. I discover new ways to appreciate both the big and small accomplishments in my daily life. Every step counts, no matter how small, and each step can help bring a more positive, harmonious life to us all.

I could choose to focus on the negative. After all, there is an abundance of that here. I could say, "It's too hot, the electricity is too expensive, I have no car, the internet is too slow, clients are never stable, almonds are insanely expensive, soy milk is $6, and I never know how much money I'll make."

But where would that get me, other than into a constant state of suffering?

So I choose to focus on gratitude.

What am I grateful for? My life. This life that I'm living right now.

I'm grateful for the friends who support and encourage me in reaching my goals. For my sweet baby kittens who are growing up so fast. For the sunshine and the rain and the warm summer days. I'm grateful that "winter" is just around the corner. For finding Lost Coast Brewery at my local supermarket. For my alternative fiber bed and the free shipping I got from Macy's and Bed Bath & Beyond. I'm grateful for days spent on the beach, letting the sound of the waves and the smell of the salty air permeate my being.

I'm grateful for the little things – the roof over my head, my yoga practice, my long term clients, having food in my fridge and my feet to get me to where I need to go. I'm grateful to have money in my bank account. I'm grateful for the Saturday feria and the good veggie market, who once looked out for me and my lost debit card for an entire week.

I'm grateful for the sun and the moon and the stars. For music and laughter and joy-filled spaces. I'm grateful to be surrounded by nature's symphony of sounds every night.

I'm grateful for the harmony and love brought into my life through my daily interactions.

These days I'm even finding gratitude for the difficult moments, for they challenge me and make me think about what I believe and how I live. I'm grateful for the ongoing life lessons.

I'm grateful for everything that has led up to this moment, both the good and the bad, the joy and the pain. It has made me into who I am, and I'm pretty happy with who I am.

I'm grateful for today, as today is fresh. Today is when I can create and cultivate my desires and my gifts.

I'm grateful for clients that fire me when we aren't a good fit, especially as it highlights my ability to stand my ground, speaking up for what I believe in. I will continue to stand up and speak up for what I believe in, no matter how many people push me down.

I'm grateful for the unknown, for that is what keeps me moving forward.

I'm grateful that I have enough courage and strength to keep putting one foot in front of the other. To keep showing up, every day, doing my work.

I'm grateful that I get to live a simple, heartfelt life. I'm grateful that I'm healthy. I'm grateful that I don't need much to be happy, and that my happiness -my contentment - is found within. It is not found in external, unreliable, or destructive sources.

I have a roof over my head. I have clothes on my body. I have a working refrigerator and someone to help me with keeping my laundry, and my house, clean. I have tile floors. I have clean, drinkable water. Most of the time I have money in my bank account to buy necessities, like groceries and cat food. I have working lights, fans and screen doors.

I am alive and breathing, and that makes me capable of just about anything.

Happiness is a way of life. Rather than seeing things as "falling apart," I see them as "falling into place." I'm living in this beautiful paradise, doing what I love, because I choose this life. And not a day goes by where I don't express gratitude for all of it.

Chapter 17

Lovingkindness

"We all are so deeply interconnected; we have no option but to love all. Be kind and do good for any one and that will be reflected. The ripples of the kind heart are the highest blessings of the Universe."

Amit Ray

Lovingkindness is a concept in Buddhism and it's the first yama in the eightfold path of Patanjali's yoga sutras (often known as non-harming/ahimsa).

But don't let that scare you off. I'm not talking about becoming Buddhist or applying different principles than what your religion already says. All of the major religions have underlying concepts that are similar to lovingkindness.

In Judaism or Catholicism, it might be: Chesed or Agape (note: while I did grow up Catholic, am sort of half Jewish and have studied Buddhism, I'm not an expert in any of these religions – while I do now like learning about religion, I kind of bombed out of World Religions 101 while at University).

When I speak about lovingkindness, I first need to look at myself. I can hardly share unconditional love with others if I'm denying it to myself.

This of course relates back to self-care as well. I can't be fully wholeheartedly loving towards others if I'm not taking care of myself. It all starts with filling myself up with love, compassion and care so that it can overflow onto those around me.

So often in the past and especially in the first few years that I lived here, I took care of others before myself. I believed the lie that it was right and noble to do so and that truly loving people did anything and everything they could for others at all times.

Let me tell you, that perspective leads to burnout and resentment. It did not improve my life or my relationships. In fact, it was a direct disservice to all involved.

Being lovingkind to myself means I give myself permission to treat myself first. You know when you're on a plane and the flight attendant says to put your air mask on before you do so for your children? That's what lovingkindness towards oneself is. Make sure you're taken care of so that can take care of others.

For me being lovingkind towards myself includes all of the self-care practices: doing my yoga or making a healthy meal or taking time to relax and listen to music or write. All of those things are lovingkind. They're all taking care of me.

But lovingkindness also goes even deeper than surface level self-care. No hour of silence or episode on Netflix compares to being actively present and acknowledging the light within me.

It is not only giving myself a free pass to splurge now and then. It's the outright expectation that I will see to my needs so that I can live up to my greatest potential, be true to my authentic self and have enough left over to see to the well-being of others.

My lovingkindness practice is generally done when I wake up, to start my day. I also use it during times of stress.

My general practice begins by intentionally cultivating the following thoughts (like a prayer or mantra) first thing in the morning.

May I be healthy
May I be happy

May I be harmonious
May I use this day to create positive ripples out into the world

Being lovingkind towards myself is more than just the saying the words above. It's about taking action on them. What I like to call: *Intentional Action*. How I show up in the world, how I present myself, how I talk to myself and to others.

I don't do negative self-talk. I know that's a popular topic these days but I generally don't put myself down. I lift myself up. I treat myself with loving kindness. I tell myself to be at peace and to be loving. To be healthy to be free. To be compassionate towards myself.

It always begins with the self. Truly we cannot offer loving kindness to others if we can't create it in ourselves first.

Once I have created a foundation of lovingkindness in myself then I can start to practice it in the world. Sometimes, it's super easy to practice: to my sweet kittens I offer loving kindness. To my friends: I offer lovingkindness. To my awesome eco wellness clients: I offer lovingkindness.

Other times, it requires a more active presence (and a few deep breaths).

At times I will offer loving kindness to people who have hurt me. This one is harder, for everyone, sometimes even on a really grounded and spiritual day. But forgiveness is a part of our daily life and offering lovingkindness is a form of forgiveness. It means that we rise above our pain and we see those who have hurt us as fellow human beings, doing the best they can with what they have at the moment. This doesn't mean that we have to label their actions good or agree with them. We simply choose to give up the position of judgment because we all have hurt and been hurt. Ideally as we get the love flowing, we move forward in our lives and we wish them all the best, health, happiness and harmony in their daily lives.

I offer lovingkindness to all the people here in Costa Rica who have taught me lessons along the way.

When I offer lovingkindness to those who have harmed me it is not so easy. It requires me to take a much deeper level of awareness into my practice. Even writing this is difficult. I can feel my heart center constricting. I can feel my breath becoming more shallow. I can sense my mind becoming congested with thoughts of the past.

The pain that I endured from my own choices and from the actions of others is within me.

The truth is that anything that happened to me in the past, I have the choice to let go of or continue to drag around with me like a dead weight.

The pain is not in the present moment, except for in my thoughts of the pain. In order to not go insane with my own stories of how life has wronged me, I choose to move through it. I choose not to suffer. I choose to instead be love and to forgive. To not think about the harm that was caused but rather how I've grown from it. What I've learned and how I can do better.

To my clients who were always asking me to do something for free, I offer lovingkindness. To the men who treat me disrespectfully either in a professional capacity because they believe women inferior or personally - who don't want to spend time getting to know me before propositioning me or who have harmed me in ways I prefer not to recount, I offer lovingkindness. To the thieves who stole not only my belongings but also the feeling of sanctuary in my home, I offer lovingkindness.

And then I extend my lovingkindness out to the environment, for it is a part of me as well. To all those in the wild environment, may they all be free, may they all be safe, may they all have plenty of food and an abundance of love.

I offer loving kindness to all the animals. All the fish in the sea who are caught, especially to the ones just used for sport; may they be healthy, may they be free, may they be alive when the hook gets taken out of them and they get thrown back in the ocean.

I offer lovingkindness to the animals because they have no voice. Because fish and cows and chickens and pigs and lambs and goats...they all have a right to be here. They all have a right to live their lives. They all have a right to grow up to have families. To love. They have that capacity in them and yet that option is taken away from them. Parents are taken away from their children. Children are taken away from their parents. So I wish them peace during their short, stunted life here on our planet.

I offer lovingkindness to our earth. May she know that we are doing our best. May she know there are people here who try to protect her. Who want to have her continue to protect us...she will be here long after we are gone. She may be burned to the ground. She may be without water. She may be without food or the ability to grow food. But she will still be here. We might not be, but she will be.

The route of lovingkindness is not always simple or easy. No road in life is paved and straight and free-flowing, no matter how many traveling salesmen offer up a snake oil potion to make it so.

I can choose to live with ease, making conscious decisions, but it is never easy. I can find ways to get through the challenges but ease and comfort rarely accompany me on those forays.

This practice has become a daily part of my life. Just like in my business or in any activity like photography or writing, the more I practice, the better I become at it. It has become a natural part of my daily life.

That is partially what lovingkindness provides me. It provides me the space to feel what I'm feeling and to move forward. To connect with my own inner light and others. It provides me with a foundation for each of my actions to be based in integrity and authenticity.

Chapter 18

Moderation

"One interesting thing about greed is that although the underlying motive is to seek satisfaction, the irony is that even after obtaining the object of your desire you are still not satisfied. The true antidote of greed is contentment."

The Dalai Lama

Costa Rica has provided me with endless opportunities to learn about moderation in my own life.

Some have been profound and some are simply daily common sense for my lifestyle, but all equally useful on my path to living, and tapping into, my inherent harmony.

In order to truly speak to moderation, I have to at least make mention of the yogi version of the principle. Brahmacharya, which is the fourth yama, from the traditional perspective means being celibate.

As a householder (a yogi living in the modern world) that is a challenge.

> Unless, of course, I actually do decide to become a female equivalent of a monk. And go live in the forest. And eat coconuts all day (some days, that sounds more and more tempting).

For this moment, becoming a monk is not in the cards and so I have to learn what moderation means to me on a personal level.

What I have found here is a lot of extremes. Drug and alcohol filled party lifestyles and promiscuity often aren't just a pass time, but a way of life.

There is also the dichotomy of those who live in

excess contrasted with that of the working poor. Very few of us even try for the middle path (though I have the whole moderation in living space covered as I live in less than 400 square feet!).

There is also the extreme of not doing anything at all. Of saying *this is good enough.*

Personally, I strive to always ask myself what good enough really even means? Am I doing as much as I possibly can? Settling for less than I'm capable of because I'm tired of the grind? Am I truly living my values?

For me, moderation is the synonym of balance. It's balancing what I do in my daily actions to ensure that I live a happy, healthy and harmonious life that then contributes to the greater good.

Life in either column of the extremes is unfulfilling. You're either depriving or overindulging. There is no quick fix nor is there any use for staying in neutral.

While I believe in being more than just "good enough", as one of my dear friends points out, we also need to understand that we are "enough".

That there is a balance between being lazy and only doing what it takes to get by and being a perfectionist and never finishing a task, project or goal for fear that it's not enough (which in turn, makes us feel that we are deficient in some way).

Since you probably read Part One already, you know that I have had sexual relationships without being in a committed monogamous relationship. At 40+ years of age, I should be able to have sex when I want. I shouldn't be prevented from having sexual relations because I don't have a committed partner...someone who I totally trust and who I want to build a future with. (I've already talked about how challenging it has been for me to find that here!)

I'm not saying that's never going to happen but at this point, since I feel like celibacy is an extreme that I have no interest in participating in, I am allowing myself to create moderation through allowing myself to have sex outside of a committed monogamous relationship. I am choosing to do that with one person rather than multiple partners. That's what makes sense to me. That reduces my risk of having health problems in the future along with problems of too many girlfriends coming after me because I slept with their cheating boyfriend (who most likely told me he was single).

I don't use drugs. I know that's not shocking, as I've shared my opinions on the subject a few times now, but it feels right to boldly proclaim my truth.

While any blanket no statement might sound like an extreme, I choose a drug free lifestyle because I'm truly not drawn to escaping my reality in that way. Doing drugs in any form would be out of balance for me, simply because it's not even something I crave, so doing so would be purely out of caving to social pressure around me. I respect myself too much to do something just because others are doing it.

I consider cigarettes, based upon their chemical content and addictive properties to be a drug. When I first moved to Costa Rica, I would occasionally smoke socially. While thankfully I don't have an addictive personality and can easily start and stop as I please, I really hate that feeling of waking up the next day, feeling miserable with a sore throat and dry mouth and just an icky smell on my body, hair, clothes and bedding.

Since my social smoking led to drinking a bit too much (which is only 2-3 glasses of wine but that's excess for me) cigarettes are pretty much out. They really are not what I want to be putting into my body.

Moderation with alcohol can look different for different people. In my own life, I am most comfortable enjoying a glass of wine when I'm done with the day. A single glass, not four. I also enjoy a cold refreshing beer at noon when it's blazing hot. I moderate my drinking because I don't want hangovers. I don't want to feel gross, to be throwing up, to not be able to get out of bed the next day, to not enjoy my life or be able to do my work because I got wasted the night before.

I'm not 16. I'm 40+. And for me, I don't want to associate with people who are still getting totally trashed. Even if it is just a few times a month. It is essentially the antithesis of everything I value and as such, I don't have much in common with people who still make that choice.

I knew someone who couldn't take his kids to school in the morning because he was too hungover. Choosing this type of lifestyle is not a mature, responsible way to conduct one's life in my opinion. Not drinking excessively is my choice. I'm not judging others. They can do whatever they want. I choose to treat my body with care.

Which brings me to food... With food I don't have an addictive personality either but because of all these weird hormonal conditions that I have going on in my body, I have to be exceptionally careful and moderate with anything that I choose to eat or drink. That is a daily practice for me.

I try not to swear. It's very rare to catch me uttering swear words, even under my breath. I think I've used one swear word in this entire book and it's really because there was just no other creative way to say what I needed to say.

I have to be extremely angry or upset to use that type of language. I know some people have a swear jar where they have to place a quarter or dollar in the jar every time they forget to mind their language. My jar would be nearly empty.

I generally have a well-balanced life. I don't watch too much TV. I don't get too much sun. Okay I probably do work too much but thankfully I enjoy the work that I do so it's not really like work for me. I love what I do. I love all the different projects that I have going on. Thankfully now (with the practices of good boundaries and authenticity in speaking my truth), I also love all my clients!

I recognize that I need to have a little bit more balance between play and work and that is something that I continue to strive for. I continue to recognize the work/life balance as a situation that needs a bit more moderation and attention to it.

I admit that I go a little crazy sometimes when people are coming down here to visit and I send them a duffel bag for them to fill with all of the boxes that I send them from Amazon and Apple and Best Buy and any other retail shop that I can possibly think of. While the full duffel bag might seem like an extreme, it's really the result of the cumulative shopping I would have done a little at a time, if I was in the US.

So I order, nearly in bulk, from the States and have a friend bring it with them. Some things, some necessary things, I can't get here or they're so expensive so I do go little crazy and excessive when I need to go shopping and someone is coming to visit.

In the beginning my plastic storage bins look like they belong to someone hoarding toiletries and such, but if I go long enough between visits, it definitely dwindles down.

At the same time, I spend barely any money here. There are very limited options and everything is so expensive. Shaving cream costs $12 for your most basic can of Gillette! You know, the short, fat ones that are probably less than $2 in the States?

Of course, for all that I value balance and moderation, sometimes I fall short of my ideals. I'm ok outing myself on this one, because it's actually kind of funny.

If I see a super cheap bag of quinoa and I know

that the price is going to go up (when they realize they either mismarked it or didn't realize how popular it was and they could make us - the foreigners - pay more) I'll buy four bags and store them in my little freezer. At one point, I had 10 bags of sunflower seeds, 10 bags of dates, 10 bags of pine nuts...all things that I cannot find in my town.

It seems crazy to me that I can't find dates and sunflower seeds and pine nuts and even sometimes quinoa (at least not for a reasonable price) but that is the reality and so I admit that I stock up a bit, perhaps excessively. On the one hand it might look greedy but on the other hand, it's very financially responsible.

Since I feel a little bad about the occasional excess foodstuffs in my home, I counter by trying to be as generous as possible when I buy these items in excess and I usually will prepare something with them and share it with my neighbors or I'll share it with visiting friends. Especially if they were the ones that picked it up for me along the way.

Living a life of moderation can sometimes be an uphill battle. We all have struggles. Sometimes we want "more" and we don't even always know why. Sometimes we live excessively.

At its core, the issue is about creating awareness and learning to be mindful of the choices that we're making. If we falter like when I smoked cigarettes or when I drank a little too much, it's tempting to beat myself up, but these days, I prefer to use those past experiences as reminders to be mindful of the circumstances that led to the situation so that I can choose differently the next time.

When we create moderation, often times, more of the things that we inherently want start to show up in our life.

Just naturally.

Living in moderation can bring us more joy as we begin to recognize the little things are truly what matter. The more that we go after things, the harder we have to work for it. You want a huge house? Then you have to put in 80 hours a week. And doesn't that take the joy out of living? Finding a balance, seeking that equilibrium in our daily life, that's what I am attempting to do.

> By living a life of moderation, I let go of the endless desire of trying to keep up with the Joneses.

I let go of never being content because I feel like there's something lacking, that there is something that I still need, something that is missing that will "make me happy" when I find it.

That is never the case, by the way. External validation is superficial at best and often times, fleeting.

Living with moderation means I make simple choices. Whether it's with my food choices or how I'm going to spend my day, nothing is too extreme. I always want to do a little more, I want to push myself a little bit further, but it's not because I lack anything. I'm content with where I am. I am mindful that I don't want to live in neutral so every day, I want to do more... I want to be more, I want to know more, I want to love and live more.

I suffer less when I live in moderation. I find that I struggle less as well.

Living a more balanced life, I can experience more happiness.

I remember that instant gratification rarely serves my highest good and that by waiting for things, sometimes it brings me even more joy when I do finally get them.

Moderation allows me to be more present and allows me to see that I'm already there. I already have everything that I need. It allows me to understand that I am enough. That what I have in my home is enough. That there isn't a necessity to live in excess.

More is not necessarily better. Even when it comes to doing yoga or meditation. Everything needs to be in balance. There needs to be equilibrium between all of the action steps that I take throughout the day and the rest that I allow to help refuel to go another day.

I'll admit that at times, I am still being pulled in too many directions at once, but by living in moderation it helps to bring my life back into balance. I am able to live more simply. I acknowledge what I want is not necessarily what I need. It also allows me to give more because I already have everything that I need.

Living in moderation is also better for the planet. If I were to buy a car, I would probably buy an SUV. But in Costa Rica where dirt roads and floods and torrential rain storms are common, I actually need one. Roads become rivers in an instant here.

Very few people though (in more modern parts of the world) actually do need a gas guzzling vehicle or a mansion for a family of four. The mess we're leaving ecologically through our obsession with "more" is absolute proof that bigger isn't always better.

As I become more mindful of my daily choices, I also am reminded that we are all connected and the way that we are living will not sustain all 7-plus billion of us. It will not sustain future generations.

By choosing to live a moderate life, I'm choosing to protect our precious planet. I believe that I am a citizen of the world, a *cosmopolitan* to quote Martha Nussbaum and the Stoic's, and I want to do everything I can to minimize my physical impact on the world while maximizing my spiritual impact.

Chapter 19
Abundance

"The key to abundance is meeting limited circumstances with unlimited thoughts."

Marianne Williamson

Abundance is like the land of possibility. This land of possibility isn't some fairy tale place like Neverland or Wonderland. It's a land of infinite opportunities in the way that the universe can prove to us that it is taking care of us and has our back.

I know you may think it's strange that it comes after moderation but once we realize that we don't need *everything* and that we can live simply what happens is that we actually find ourselves living a more abundant life.

Here's how I have found more abundance in my life. By living more simply, I am definitely more mindful. Abundantly mindful. I bring mindfulness into my daily life by doing simple tasks that I used to automate.

I don't like doing the dishes but I now bring mindfulness to doing the dishes because I don't have a dishwasher. And I only have one small sink, not two large ones as I did in California. I bring mindfulness to my daily tasks and it creates more of an abundance because I am more present and aware of each moment.

Presence creates more love and joy and harmony and peace in my life. It isn't about the things that I have (although I would prefer that they not get stolen) but it is about creating experiences and moments in my daily life that are meaningful. That is what creates abundance in my life.

By being able to have these wildhearted experiences, my life is full of abundance. It's full of goodness and joy and love. It's full of kittens running around playing, their eyes lighting up whenever I go to give them a treat or when a gecko runs across the floor. Ah, the abundance of simple joy and simple pleasures.

Abundance for me is not about how many black dresses I have or how many pairs of shoes or sunglasses or hats. It's not about how much money is in my bank account. Because really, the money is always there. Especially when I live more simply.

Recognizing what I already have and feeling deep gratitude for it creates a richness in my life that I could not possibly gain by spending and having more. Living with abundance allows me to give more generously, which creates more abundance in wholehearted ways that are not only a benefit for me, but for all.

So how do I create abundance? All depends on the moment. It depends on what I want to be abundant in. On some days that are exceptionally bad, I hope for an abundance of laughter and happiness and of someone being kind or generous or simply reaching out. Even just sending me a virtual hug adds to my abundance of things to be grateful for.

Living in moderation, nothing is in excess. Either positive or negative. There needs to be a balance.

With abundance, there is also a dark side, one that many people fear. The opposite of abundance is scarcity: the feeling that there never has been and never will be enough to go around.

The notion of scarcity can be terrifying for

people. Scarcity might mean I don't have enough food, I don't have enough money to buy food, I don't have money to fix my roof leak. I don't have enough money to pay my rent. Scarcity is a scary place to live.

I'm familiar with scarcity. It is definitely not a fun pair of goggles through which to view life. Sort of brown and dismal colored as opposed to rosy.

Being an independent consultant and a one income family, when I've lost clients, that can tempt me to play the awful scarcity "what if" game. What if I lose all of my clients, can't pay my rent, have to give up my cats and end up homeless in another country far away from any type of support system?!?

The thought is based on the belief that there are only so many clients in the world and I need to keep every single one of them, no matter the fit. The truth is that the same Universe that brought me a client can bring me another... or another twelve, but if I dip into the scarcity mindset it's a bit like saying *"No, no Universe, don't help. I'm gonna strive, struggle and suffer my way to one new client. Thanks for your offer, but I've got this."*

In reality all losing a client means is that I need to make a shift. Scarcity is just a fear tactic. Something we can get lost in and feel completely paralyzed by. That is not how I want to feel.

Thank goodness I know that I have a choice. I get to choose whether I want to live with abundance or scarcity.

Fortunately, somehow, when I choose to live with abundance, to see my life through an abundant lens, scarcity goes away. That extrinsic fear goes away. I know it's outside of me. Something always shows up to replace the client that left or I find some other way to make things work. I've always said if I have to eat rice and beans every day, I will eat rice and beans every day. I will make this life work for me.

When I look back at my life, I can see how the universe has listened and provided. Almost every job I've ever wanted (even those which I was totally under-qualified for), I've gotten. And every client I've really wanted, I've also gotten. Not always right away...some took a few weeks or months, one took 3 years! But I also believe that everything happens when it's supposed to happen.

> The universe truly does have an abundance to give. But it is up to me to trust and be grateful for all of the opportunities that surround me.

By continuing to move forward and opening myself up to all that is possible, life will provide me with infinite gifts. I have to be open to be receiving and say thank you when they inevitably arrive.

What I do:

Appreciate all that I have.

Give compliments freely.

Connect with those I care about.

I act like a child in the most mature but

awestruck, wonder wall way.

I go after what I want. I get out of the stuck and neutral-living patterns. I know that I'll never know what I can do if I don't try.

I set my intentions and maintain them through my words and my actions.

I find ways of living that create an abundance of pure joy and contentment.

Abundance of love and peace. Having nothing to do with the amount of money in my bank account or how many pairs of shoes are in my closet.

> There is an abundance of life
> to be lived.

Chapter 20
Authenticity

"The privilege of a lifetime is to become who you truly are."

C.G. Jung

When we choose to lie, cheat, manipulate, steal, it causes harm to oneself: one's body, mind and spirit, as it is not in alignment with the truth of our being. It also causes harm to others—those you have been disingenuous towards and those who you have spoken untruthfully about.

We cause destruction in our world when we choose to lie, even if it is just a "little white lie". We can use our words to cause destruction—in ourselves and our families and communities—or we can use our words to create messages of inspiration, hope and joy.

> We can speak truthfully, using positive language, and create inspiring actions.

When we tell lies or act in an inauthentic manner, we're trying to avoid pain, either our own or someone else's. While it may avoid some pain, on a deeper level, lies and insincerity keep us in a state of suffering. It doesn't allow us to grow when we're not being truthful, either with ourselves or others.

A lot of times, we numb the pain, either by telling more lies, continuing with misaligned actions, or turning to actual depressants like drugs or alcohol to help us desensitize our daily life and our daily troubles as well as our inauthentic actions. I've had quite a few times when people who had lied or not fulfilled their commitments try to put the situation back on me, as if their inactions and inability to do as they said was my fault.

Occasionally, when I've wanted to confront someone about dropping the ball on a leg of a project, I've been told that I couldn't because it would make them feel bad. But wouldn't the truth set us all free?

If we could tell these people that they messed up their section of the project (which in turn messed up my section), then they could take responsibility for their actions and fix the problem which would then allow me to proceed with my job. Similarly, if I'm the one in the wrong, I want to know so that I can take ownership, fix the problem and free everyone to go on with their own work.

I find great freedom in the truth.

Whenever possible, I model the personal and professional relationships that I would like to engage in. I'm not going to say this has been easy or that I've actually succeeded 100% of the time. I have definitely had moments when I've been dragged down into the muck and given back what I've been given, rather than what I would like to receive. Welcome to being human.

I do try to show up in a way that is aligned with my values. It's actually not always appreciated.

I've been told that when I live my values, I come off as acting superior. Unfortunately, that's a fairly human dynamic. Ask any straight A student, or kid accused of being a goodie-two-shoes. People infinitely prefer when we conform to their standards, rather than maintain our own.

The good news is that other people don't get to define my existence. As I step into authentic living more fully, I let go of clients that would ask something less of me and attract those whose values align with mine.

Trusting myself enough to get past the naysayers can be hard work. It required knowing myself, the core of who I am, and being willing to let people dislike me which can be hard in a people pleasing culture.

I don't see many around me, willing to stand their ground in the face of disapproval from others. I would venture to say it's one of the reasons so little innovation takes place and everything moves at a sloth's pace.

So few that I've met are empowered to actually believe in themselves, know who they are and are willing to do the work necessary to live a totally fulfilling, wildhearted life.

I see this as all the more reason why I am here, doing what I do and trying to be the best role model I can be.

There is a beautiful simplicity in that goal. Because when I show up in an authentic way, then all my thoughts, words and actions are in alignment and working for the greater good. What I intend to do and what I actually do are 100% in sync and supporting one another. There is nothing to be afraid of; no repercussions. And isn't that a beautiful way to show up in the world?

My choice of authenticity allows me

CHRISSY GRUNINGER

to live freely, without fear.

When we lie, either to ourselves or others, we are not acting in our truest nature and it creates, in us, a less than pure state. The light of our divine spirit, our inherent harmony, begins to diminish. Whether the lie comes to light or not and whether we want to admit it or not, it creates a divide in ourselves and in our relationships, draining our energy. When we speak anything less than the truth, we're always having to watch our back, never knowing when it will catch up to us or what repercussions will come from it.

When we shy away from honesty with others because it might hurt their feelings, we do a disservice to ourselves and them.

For example, I had a friend who refused to simply tell his girlfriend that he needed a little space and wanted to engage in fewer phone conversations. Instead he made up lies to get off the phone. His space needs weren't met and she had no idea that he felt she was being too needy and clingy. A typical lose-lose created by a lie to preserve her feelings.

While the truth may not always be the easiest way to go, it is the only way that produces freedom.

At the risk of throwing said friend under the bus, I have to examine another lie of his for its relationship damaging effects. Though his girlfriend (who was long distance) was coming to visit in a week, he propositioned me, not wanting to wait that long. He saw a female body in front of him and it was what he wanted, in that moment. In addition to the instant gratification inherent in this story, it also speaks to some commitment issues. I'm not saying that the simple fact that he wanted to have sex with someone out of his relationship makes him a bad person. I'm simply inviting us all to imagine how the relationship could have been devastated by the lie and infidelity (don't worry, I turned him down flat) and conversely to think about how having an honest conversation about their wants and needs might have strengthened their relationship. How can your partner help give you what you want and need when you never speak to those needs?

He wanted me to meet his girlfriend during her visit but I told him no because I was uncomfortable being a part of his lies. If she happened to ask me something that I knew he had lied about to her, I would have told her the truth.

"If you propose to speak, always ask yourself: Is it true? Is it necessary? Is it kind?"

This well-known quote (attributed to Buddha, but not accurately), is a good reference point for living an authentic life. The one that always gets me tripped up is the last one, *"Is it kind?"*. And I suppose it would depend on the situation. The truth can hurt but it can also set us free. So is it not kind because it hurts or is it indeed kind because it sets you free? Something I continue to work through... I definitely do not have all the answers.

Becoming more aware of authenticity and how it shows up in my life is a mindful task. Being honest with myself and others can be uncomfortable. But when truth shows up, beauty is created. Not only in my own life but in the lives of all.

I get to build relationships, rather than tear them down. I get to manifest positive reactions rather than negative. I get to feel whole, rather than divided.

Authenticity allows me to live my truth and not have to worry about remembering lies that I've told and who I told them to. (or remember them for my friends, as in the case above)

Authenticity provides us with the opportunity to build up from the depths and relight the spark in each other.

When I witness how I'm showing up in the world, my goal is for it to always be with a genuine spirit that is true to my inherent nature.

Living my truth is at the very core of who I am. When I speak, I choose my words with care. And even then, sometimes, it may still hurt the other person.

When my words are dictated by my truth and inherent harmony, the intention is to be of service, not cause harm. If I speak with kindness and truth, and the receiver feels harmed, chances are that it's their own insecurities which are causing them pain, not my words.

In Business

When I write a contract for a new account, I am very intentional about the included line items. I know that I am capable of completing them and the time it will roughly take me to finish. I'm also very specific about the types of work I provide.

Sometimes it seems silly to think of that as such a necessity. When a plumber comes over, most people are unlikely to ask them to take a look at their oven which isn't heating correctly.

Unfortunately, as a marketing consultant and happiness mentor, not everyone is as clear on the services that I provide, so I have to spell my services out as clearly as possible. I also note that requests for work outside the scope of the contract will be considered and billed separately, in case someone comes up with something in my wheelhouse that we hadn't thought of at the outset.

It's kind of amusing to me how many people have signed my contract, initialed next to that special section and still want me to show up and do work that is totally outside of what we do. For FREE. One client, after the contract was signed, wanted me to work in his database and be a reservations agent. My contract is clear – I do marketing, not sales. It's not that I couldn't do it. I didn't want to do it. Unlike so many others who say Yes, when they mean No, I am really clear on what I want to do in my life and my business. And

I have no problem expressing that.

In this case, asking me to do admin work (and god help me, sales, something I truly despise) in a database is not a good use of my skills or my time. I'm certainly qualified, but just because you're good at something doesn't mean you have to say Yes to doing it when someone asks. I recommended that his sales team handle such requests, an idea that went nowhere, despite its total validity. In the meantime, I was being told that I wasn't a team player since I wouldn't do the work for free.

When we're practicing our truth, when we're really showing up as our most truthful selves, that's when our Right Livelihood becomes a reality. And that's honestly what I'm striving for. Sales and databases and telling individual people about the hotel's rooms is *not* what I want to do. And no one can make me if I'm clear about my boundaries.

As a marketing consultant, I get to reach out, tell stories and touch the lives of many, not just a few. I might show you a picture of the room with a gorgeous ocean view, but I don't want to provide you with the minute details of what's inside it, how much it costs, how many people can stay in the room, is breakfast included, is there a mini-frig, what's inside it, etc.

Being authentic means we show up in a truthful way. I don't lie and say I can do something when I can't (or in this case above, don't want to). Whether it's a task that we don't know how to do or a social engagement that we don't really want to attend, we're only hurting ourselves and the others involved when we give a Yes that is less than full bodied.

I also don't want to just sit on a mat and let that be my mindfulness practice. I want to *do* something. And if that means speaking up against incompetence in a room full of sexist men, then so be it. They may choose to not actually "hear" me, and to digest my words, but at least I know I've taken a step towards living an authentic life with integrity. I'm not responsible for their response of comprehension, just my own output of my truth. That's always within my control.

I show up as "me" whether people think I should or not, whether it's accepted by the majority or not and even it gets me fired.

Getting fired by the wrong client is actually a gift. They free up my time and energy to find clients with whom I have more synergy and as a natural byproduct of that synergy, more fun working with as well. That is another beautiful gift of living authentically.

I am a whole being, I stand for courage, for a balanced world, one where we are all equal.

When I can truly express myself, being open and vulnerable, it provides me with a sense of freedom. Of contentment. Of wildhearted living. Stress and anxiety don't creep up on me when faced with little bumps in the road. They just don't bother me anymore. I can even, sometimes, laugh at them.

The path of authenticity

Feelings are natural. We each have them. When we repress them, we lose our true self, our true nature. Expressing them is only uncomfortable if I allow it to be. Whether it's popular or not, I will stay true to myself. I will express myself, be seen and recognized for who I am, what I do and how I show up in the world.

Authenticity allows me to feel confident and secure in my daily life, it allows me to show up as myself, my true nature, it allows me to be more present, more positive, more assertive and knowledgeable about what my true intentions are.

What does showing up authentically look like?

My core values are defined. My thoughts, words and actions are equally aligned. I stay focused on the present moment. Each step I take, when in alignment with my values, helps me stay on the path and brings me more into the light.

Sometimes I fall off the path. I show up in an inauthentic way. But I get up, brush myself off and examine what happened, why it happened and then I continue on the path with this new knowledge. Each time, it gets a little easier. I have found it takes so much more energy when I'm living inauthentically, so it's draining and less fun... Another lose-lose.

The other (somewhat) amusing point here is I've

always been the type of person to go to bat for others. To speak up on the behalf of others who may not always have a voice. I'm not only talking about animals here, like monkeys and cows. I'm talking about people who I've worked with who seem to get the short end of the stick.

If they're trying their best, doing their work, and showing up yet get mistreated despite their efforts, I'm often the first in line to come to their defense. Since I've been in management roles since I was in high school, I've often been in a position to stand up for other team members because I knew how hard they were working and how little they received in return.

Authenticity means I show up as ME.

When a client I worked with wanted me to become someone that I was not, wanted me to pretend to be someone I was not, I refused.

You know what happens when you start pretending to be someone you're not? You lose yourself.

I have worked too hard to be told that I have to change and mold to make other people like me. If, at the end of the day, I still like me and feel aligned with my values, I'm willing to handle a little dislike or disapproval from others who don't get me.

Chapter 21

Wildhearted Harmony

"You only live once but if you do it right, once is enough."

Mae West

Everyone deserves to live a fulfilling, empowered, happy, healthy, and harmonious life, to thrive in the freedom created by the choices they make. That looks different for every individual, because we each have our own paths. And yet, we are also all totally connected.

It was as I finally reached the step of wildhearted harmony that the rug got swept out from under me. Again.

As I write that, I'm actually smiling and laughing a little. It was like the universe was once again giving me a test. I understood that I needed to surrender, accept, grow, actively pursue self-care, be lovingkind and grateful, and to live simply with moderation. I learned that by doing so, abundance would appear and authenticity would deepen, which would then lead to a wildhearted life.

I diligently plotted and took all of those steps, found myself and got back on the path.

I was fulfilled. I was connected to community around the world, beautiful souls wanting to do more with their lives, wanting to lift each other up. I finally felt like I was experiencing a wildhearted life... and then the rug got swept out from under me.

And I had to return to the steps once again. I picked myself back up, brushed myself off and started breathing into each moment. I once again had to let go of something that I held dear, something that I really believed in. Some things aren't meant to be, no matter how badly we might crave the experience or security we think they will bring us.

I thought I had found my most ideal perfect client but I was reminded that perfection is a result of detachment from outcome, rather than fulfilling my expectations to the letter.

My expectations, while they have the opportunity to cause me to feel let down, also serve as reminders of my boundaries (when they are crossed) and my ability to choose where I go, what I do and what I will say.

There are certain things that do not go together: oil and water, my work ethic and the laid back deadline free culture I live in, my belief in valuing individuals regardless of race, gender, etc and Costa Rica's wariness of outsiders or those who don't fit into a specific mold.

I knew that I would get back to my wildhearted harmony, even faster than the last time since I now had a framework of steps. I trusted that I would feel fulfilled again and that gaps in that feeling were momentary and to be expected.

They call it a practice for a reason. If I ever find myself off course (which as a human being is inevitable), I have only to re-engage the practice of tapping into my inherent harmony to bring myself back to wildhearted bliss.

I know the importance of being present in every moment, even if sometimes it's a tall order. Best of all, I know that other people don't have to understand my life or "get" my choices.

> This is my ONE wild and beautiful life and I don't have to settle for what other people value.

As long as I bring consciousness to my decisions rather than flailing about like a 16 year old hoping to move up in the high school hierarchy of popularity, I can create a life that I am proud of and happy to live.

I will make mistakes and occasionally trade my inherent harmony for dissatisfaction, discontent and disillusionment. It can be very alluring for a time until you realize what you've lost. It's that moment that reminds me to get back on the path.

Life will throw us some serious curveballs, just to test our ability to choose peace.

I know that has been especially true for me since moving to Costa Rica. It has definitely not been all "pura vida". And with every challenge I become stronger. I admit, it's hard doing it with a global rather than local support system. But I'd rather be on my own than have to be something I'm not.

The challenge:
It's hard to be present when I feel like the world is crashing down around me and everything is a mess.

The solution:

To dig deep. To show up. To do the work. To make my thoughts, words and actions all equal each other. That is how I can truly live in harmony.

I have to dig so deep sometimes, into my soul, and utilize the practices that I've been doing now for 20+ years (with 15 years of focused dedication). This is how I find my harmony, my wildhearted living, it is rarely easy but I can find ease by staying in the present, taking a few deep breaths and knowing that this too shall pass.

> While choosing peace can be difficult in the midst of chaos, the fact remains that the steps to harmony remain simple.

Finding my breath always brings me back to the present moment. It brings me back to why I am here. Fueled with my passionate desire to be of service and make a difference, I remember why I make the choices, even when curling up in fetal position and pitching a temper tantrum sounds like more fun.

To be honest, even with all the craziness, very few tears have been shed during my life in Costa Rica. In all the years I've been here, I've only had two or three total breakdowns: sitting in the shower crying my eyes out as the water falls over me, another time yelling at someone at 3 o'clock in the morning because I couldn't understand the insanity of the situation that was taking place. I'm not proud of that moment but I can't take back the past.

I can only be here in the present and do better.

It seems like only two isn't enough for all of the challenges that I've experienced in the last few years but those are the only two that still I remember and someday maybe even those will be a distant memory that I won't even try to reflect on because there's nothing left to learn from them. Hey, a girl can hope!

If there was a third time when I completely lost it, I don't remember anymore.

Well, there was that time in the bank manager's office but come on, 18 months to open a business bank account? You'd be crying too.

Isn't it funny how something that seems so important in the moment can fade and you can't even dredge the story back up? That's freedom.

My goal is to understand more and be more loving, open, forgiving and aware of the notion that everyone is doing the best they can with what they have at the time.

Sure, I might not like someone's best (or my own sometimes) but judgment isn't the way forward. Love is.

Even though I felt lost through most of the first few years of living here, deep down intrinsically, inside of me, my inherent harmony was always there. The steps don't create inherent harmony... they allow you to return to it.

Our Inherent Harmony is always there and it's our job to return to love as often as necessary.

All of the work that I've done has enabled me to be stronger and to be more present and to be able to live fully in the moment and to accept what is and to let go of what I cannot change.

I know I sound like the serenity prayer. Don't knock it. That simple prayer is chock full of arrows pointing the way to harmony. There's a reason some people say it every day.

Where do I go now?

I have all that I need in this moment. I don't know what I'll be doing in five years. I don't know where I'll be in 15 years. I've joked that if I can't make it work in Costa Rica, I'm moving to Cuba.

Now that changes have been made to the embargo and new regulations are being put into place, it's at least a possibility. Or maybe I'll go to Nicaragua. I have a friend that thinks Thailand would be the ideal place for me. According to her it has the same environment but is a much more cost effective place to live. Who knows, maybe you'll end up with my memoir of experiences in Thailand as my next book.

I don't know what the future holds and I don't need to. I only know that I'm here in this moment.

The present moment is where change and growth occur.

I know I need to show up and do the work. I know I need to go deeper into my practice. I know that I am love and I know that I am loved.

Every day that I am here I get to do more. I get

to show up. I get to be, to learn.

New opportunities are always coming into my life. I believe that happens because I have this inherent harmony in me allowing me enough space to expand out, to give more, receive more, do more and be more. That is what Wildhearted Harmonious living is.

Wildhearted Harmony is living the life that you want to live in a way that serves all. It is being a citizen of the world. It is recognizing that we are all one, connected and inseparable, though we may look different, believe in different things and make different choices.

When you understand how your unique gifts and talents can be of service to the world, you get to show up doing what you love while making a difference. It's not about being selfish, looking out for only yourself, but rather creating situations where there are no losers.

Wildhearted harmony is about living in harmony with myself and others and the world around me. It doesn't mean that everyone needs to love me or that I need to take care of everyone.
I am not a saint.

It means that I simply need to show up as my highest, truest self and to do what comes naturally from a place of love. When I give as generously as I can, respecting others ability to love and live, I am able to live from the heart, wildly and free.

Generosity of spirit lends itself to giving of my time, experience, money, clothes and talent. It can also be as simple as being more present with my clients. It's not always about doing more, but rather BEING exactly who I am at my core.

There is no reason to settle for anything less than what my soul desires to bring forth into the world. In matters of passionate service, there is no such thing as "good enough", just my best.

I don't really believe in reincarnation. I believe we get this one life and if we happen to get another one then that's all fine and well, but it doesn't relieve me of the responsibility for rocking this one.

I'm living for today. My hope is to make harmonious living possible for all. I want to create wellness and equality in our communities, in our lives, in our families, for the earth.

My highest aim is to let every thought, word and action that I create be in harmony with the greater good.

To live my life fully and not look back on it and find wasted moments, breaths and experiences.

I want to leave the earth an even better place than how I found it. I strive to continue to be mindful of the choices that I make. To continue to learn about other cultures and how we can all get along.

That is wildhearted harmonious living.

I want the world to come to a deep understanding of the fact that our apparent differences (race, gender, orientation, beliefs, you name it) don't actually make us separate.

The same energy of love courses through my veins as does yours. To be concerned about the appearance of separateness is to miss the heart of the matter. Who we are, how we show up says more about us than anything you can tell about us from a glance. To continue to work towards respecting each other, knowing that we're each here to do something, to do something good for ourselves and for others - that is wildhearted harmonious living.

When I know myself, to my core, and allow my inherent harmony to work outward from my heart, I am able do more and create more because I'm no longer wasting time judging or doubting myself.

We are all created purposefully and when we live into a space of using our time, talents and treasure to be of passionate service, we are able to see the miraculous in even the smallest of moments.

The temptation to play the blame game, with ourselves or others, keeps us from being all that we can be (even in the Army, not that I've ever had a desire to join.)

I believe that we are each beautiful harmonious beings. We are made up of light and love. We all have cells and tissues and muscles and bones and blood. We may have a few different organs but we are still all human, all equal, all living on this one planet.

We are connected to the sun and the moon and the stars. We can see the direct connections as the moon affects our tides or when there is both sunshine and rain, a rainbow appears. When there is light, you know there will be dark.

There are some truths in our world that we can't not see. And those truths include that we are all here for a reason, we are all love, we are all One.

By living a wildhearted life, being sanguine, I am able to better see how we are all interconnected.

We are not just one with each other but ONE with all of life.

We're connected to the trees and the flowers and the hummingbirds and the bees. We're connected to the wildlife that's running around on the forest floor or high up in the canopy. We're connected to the butterflies and the birds. We're connected to all that we see and all that we don't see.

We're connected not only to the farmers but to their land. To the land that they're caring for that's providing us with the food that nourishes our bodies.

We're connected to the people who make our clothes, to the people who make the furniture in our home. We're connected to those who build cars or bus drivers or taxi drivers or who make the sidewalks that we walk on. We're connected to the mail carrier (for those of us who actually get mail), we're connected to people in faraway lands who make all the products that we use on a daily basis.

All of these people provide support to us in one way or another, whether we think of them or not.

And, living wildheartedly, all of these connections cause us to feel a profound sense of gratitude for our life and the lives of all other beings in our world. It's just so beautiful.

I give back and pay it forward as I continually work to understand the connections that are present throughout the world. It doesn't require that I travel to these countries, I can do this just through my simple gratitude and lovingkindness practices.

But when I do travel to different countries and see who the people are that live there and how they live, what they eat, how they go to school, what their family life is like, I recognize the interconnections and remember, we are all One.

It may not look like my life. It may not look like what I think is normal. But wildhearted harmony tells me that each of us is perfectly imperfect and none of us have any room to judge.

If I see someone acting in a way that doesn't align with what I believe to be right, I don't have to condemn them. Perhaps I speak up or if that's not an option, I can always let it be a moment that causes me to reflect on how *I* show up in the world.

If I see someone acting unfairly, I can reflect on the times that I have been unfair and pay attention to how my choices affect the world around me, rather than labeling that other person bad and going about my day with a sense of "at least I'm not crappy like *them*".

In a state of wildhearted harmony, there truly is no "other". What I see in others, I can find in myself, both positive and negative. It is my responsibility to use this feedback to move forward in love.

I know that for me, the reality is that living here has been difficult. I find it difficult to accept the choice of parents to kick out a 14-year-old pregnant girl once the baby arrives. That is not my idea of love, generosity or a reflection of what I value. I can't make the choice for them and it might not even be my place to speak to them, but I can absolutely look at the places in my own life where I have acted unlovingly or in discord with my values. I can go back and make amends or at least vow to choose differently going forward.

Every moment has value, even if I find it difficult to see immediately.

I also find it difficult to see people who live in homes with dirt floors. But I've to come to understand that is what is normal for them.

It's especially challenging to deal with being automatically disliked because of the color of my skin or others' belief that my gender makes me less worthy.

It's difficult to be seen as a physical object

rather than as a living breathing human being with a mind and heart and soul.

These moments provide me with an amazing amount of empathy for the lives of so many people who experience this type of discrimination in their own home country.

It is an experience that few people of my background experience but that I wish more had access to. I imagine it would breed a whole lot more compassion, connection and desire to do right by our fellow human beings.

It's difficult to be around people who don't have the same morals, values or ethics and to still see them as connected to me; to still give them lovingkindness. But Oneness isn't just true for the people I like and understand. It is the truth for all life and these differences help show me my own path in a way that I may not always find comfort in but for which I do find exceptional gratitude.

This is a part of my daily, continuous practice. This is wildhearted harmony. It's not always easy, it's not always pretty. It's life. And life is messy and chaotic and, well, wild at times. I wouldn't have it any other way.

My happy place

Here I've created my happy place.

My happy place is being healthy, it's playing with the kittens, it's enjoying the sunshine and the sandy beach at sunrise, it's going to the farmers market, it's talking with friends on Skype. It's a very simple life.

It doesn't necessarily look like other people's happy place. And that's because it's mine.

I'm finding a balance between play and work. I'm creating a balance every day between giving and receiving, making sure that I'm being taking care of, making sure that I'm not being taken advantage of or manipulated.

Do I want more? Yes and no. At this moment, I'm happy. Or really, I'm sanguine. Do I think that there's more ahead for me? Most definitely...because I'm going to create it.

I create my happy place in every moment. I create the moments in my life that make or create or build more harmony.

It is not always perfect and it doesn't always turn out the way I hope it will but then I remember I must be willing to shift and change and realize that there's a better day ahead of me tomorrow.

My values never shift but my expectations and hopes for outcomes often do as I'm presented with more information.

Where to next?

I feel like I'm 22 here. Maybe it was because I was so sick in California that I'm now reliving my youth but I really do feel so young. Young at heart, in spirit, in mind and in body. Life is just beginning and each day is a fresh start.

Thanks to my awareness of the steps to inherent harmony and my ability to actively engage them in any moment, who I am now, versus the "lost" me during those first 900 or so days, is a much more accurate and authentic representation of me.

There is still more work to be done. More fun to be had. More experiences, good and bad, in front of me. But having found my *sanctuary within, my inherent harmony* means I get to expand out in new and beautiful ways. It means I continue on my path with more stability, security and an innate sense that all is well, even when it's falling apart.

More wildhearted living lies ahead for me and I'm choosing to proceed fearlessly, secure in the knowledge that my peace is generated from within, rather than without.

Right now, I can only do as much as I'm doing and then push a little harder. When I get pushed down or back (as I often do), I simply have to pick myself back up.

For me, to truly live in a wildhearted way, I have to know that for today I have succeeded. I have done what I set out to do. I have lived a life that is in harmony for all. I have stated my intentions and am actively working towards them.

I have created the life that I want to live.

I'm living in the present moment.

I'm not worried about the future because I have no control over what lies ahead.

I can only control my choices in the present

moment and in this moment, I choose to live in Costa Rica, in my happy place, to be present and create the most harmonious beautiful vibrant life I can imagine.

And it's all just the beginning...

I'm happy where I am. I'm not constantly looking for the gold at the end of the rainbow. I'm just grateful for the rainbow. I'm grateful for both the rain and the sunshine that created the rainbow. The good and the bad, the light and the dark, it all exists together. I acknowledge both but focus on the positive outcome.

You may call it taking the good with the bad, finding the silver lining, the bright side or the pot of gold.

I call it making rainbows, pot of gold or no pot of gold.

Living here has forced me out of any type of comfort zone that I thought existed. Normal does not exist here. At least not my version of it.

Being uncomfortable allows me to not just survive, but thrive. To embrace the discomfort and work through it.

My mindfulness practice has really been a useful aid. It allows me to be present with what is but I also know that the tide will eventually shift and I will overcome any loss, painful event or frustration that I am faced with.

At my core, I am the same person that I was when I moved here. I am the same person and yet I'm not. I've grown, I've changed. I've let go.

What's changed is that I know who I am on an even deeper level. I'm stronger, more resilient and living a much more wildhearted life than when I arrived.

I have spent an extraordinary amount of time on my own (almost like I did become that monk living in a shack at the beach) reflecting and rejuvenating.

I've gotten to know more of who I am, what I want, what my core values, beliefs and principles are. This quality time alone has allowed me to really slow down, to be present with myself and to open up in new ways to the outside world. It has allowed me to reorient myself, into new ways of thinking, doing and being.

It has not been easy.

The "being alone" part, that's not the problem. It's the sitting with all these challenges and strange things that happen and trying to make some sense of it all, how it fits into my life. Without making myself or my friends abroad crazy.

Learning how I can come out on the other side a better, healthier, happier and more harmonious person.

I have learned that things might change...and they might not. Status quo, mindlessly swimming with the stream, is accepted here more often than not. To its demise, in my opinion.

But I keep choosing to mindfully swim

upstream, believing every choice I make creates a positive ripple. Reaching near and far.

We are each here for a reason. Every small step we take, every mindful action, makes a difference.

I am an active participant in my life. I don't accept the status quo for myself. I'm not living in neutral. I am always growing, learning, blossoming, and letting go when the time is right.

I have had to learn how to live in a totally different culture, and still be me.

I've realized that my life may not look like your life. And guess what? In my book, that's totally okay. So you let me be me and I'll let you be you. I'm living my ONE beautiful life, *my way*. Isn't that what Ol' Blue Eyes said?

THE END

LOST AND FOUND IN THE LAND OF MAÑANA

CHRISSY GRUNINGER

EPILOGUE

LOST AND FOUND IN THE LAND OF MAÑANA

CHRISSY GRUNINGER

the present moment
December 2016

Be simply sanguine: Empowered to thrive in an imperfect world.

I can honestly say now that I am in love with my life. The good and the bad. Sure, there are still things that bother me about living here: the high cost of living (*for Costa Rica*); the ongoing discrimination; and the lack of real, deep connections with people who have similar beliefs and values as myself.

But there's so much more that I love. I'm creating a wildhearted life every single day. It's fulfilling, meaningful and adventurous.

I said in the beginning that we all choose to stay, for one reason or another. So why do I stay? Beyond the year-round summertime? And good health?

As I write this, it's nearly 2 years after I wrote the final chapter, Wildhearted Harmony. It's the end of the rainy season; the days are warm and sunny with cooler nights. I am now living in that little shack at the beach. It even has mango and banana trees, coconut palms and... get this... a yellow lemon tree.

Thank You Universe.

From my covered patio, I watch as lightning bolts light up the sky and the rain falls with determination. A migrating Oriole is taking shelter under a large leaf on the papaya tree.

At other times, I'm mesmerized by the golden flicker of fireflies dancing amongst the trees. I'm woken up by the sound of a flock of parrots and drift off to sleep to the harmonious orchestral offerings of cicadas, crickets and frogs.

I continue to live in the present. I notice the man who sweeps the leaves from the road every day but only puts them off to the curb, so every night the leaves are blown back into the street by wind or rain or just a car driving by a little too quickly. But he's there, every day. Rain or shine.

Someone down the road is yelling, "*Upe!*" And I know I'll hear the call of, "*Pancito!*" in the morning.

My business is thriving. And as I'm a multi-passionate entrepreneur, my second business of mentoring others to live their ONE beautiful life on their own terms is also starting to pick up speed and I couldn't be happier. This is what I'm here to do - creating harmony out in the world both for individuals and professionals.

Friends come to visit and bring me large duffel bags of supplies. They set me up for the next 6-12 months with shaving cream, toothbrushes, soap, vegan protein powder and whatever else I might be running low on that either I can't find or it's too expensive to buy here.

Rumors abound about me. Some think I've left the country. Some have told me that they thought I got married. Others heard I was pregnant. I roll my eyes and smile, this is real life on the Rich Coast.

I still don't understand the people who come to live here and want to sit at the beach all day and do nothing other than drink and use drugs but I know not to judge. That's their life and their choice.

Sunshine and Lluvia, my two adorable, somewhat wild, adopted children are furry bundles of playfulness and total unconditional love. While fully grown now, they still act like kittens.

Sunshine loves everyone and drools instead of purrs when he's pet. Lluvia seems to dislike all men. She's also terrified of the rain and coconuts. But she absolutely loves having her belly rubbed.

They watch the birds play in the trees, the jesus christ lizards scurry on the ground and the monkeys eating the mangos. They are always super excited when a creature (frog, dragonfly, butterfly, gecko and yes, even gigantic cockroaches), find their way into the house.

There are a lot of tail-less geckos running around as a result of their youthful enthusiasm.

Thankfully, we have not yet had any incidences with scorpions and should we ever, I'm extremely grateful that their vet makes house calls and lives just up the road. We did have one caterpillar (which can be highly toxic) but I got to it before they did. I'm not entirely convinced that they appreciated my efforts, but such is the life of a pet mom.

The last time I wore jeans was before moving here in 2012. A few times a year when a tropical storm comes through with cooler wind, I do need to dig out my socks and yoga pants. But it's a rare occasion.

Besides flip flops, I haven't worn real shoes in, well, a few years now. I think the last time I wore hiking boots or sneakers was when I traveled to Cerro de la Muerte to see the resplendent quetzal in 2014.

I've talked with people in the US in wintertime who tell me they are just starting to hear the birds sing again in the morning as spring approaches and I realize how blessed I am to have the songs of birds enliven my everyday life.

I haven't been sick since January 2013. No colds, no flu, nada. I still have allergies sometimes but only when I'm in a cold, dry environment. Or on winter days when my indoor house temperature drops below 81°F.

I have the funniest conversations with my regular taxi drivers. I could probably write a little e-book just about that. Think: *Taxi Cab Confessions, Costa Rica Style.* One of them always shares whatever snacks he has with him at the time – I love the homemade plantain chips.

I continue to learn how to make my own lip balm, sugar scrub and coconut milk. I've also become quite the raw food chef.

I have sun-kissed skin and natural golden highlights in my hair.

In contrast to my life in California, I've traded taking visitors to wineries for a tour at the National Park with one of my good friends who is truly the best guide (and birder) in the region.

I've traded a dishwasher, dryer, hot water and garbage disposal to live next to a tree full of scarlet macaws and three different types of monkeys.

The rugged, but oh so cold, Northern California coastline has been traded for tropical blue, 85-degree water.

The 200-foot redwood trees in the temperate forest have been replaced with the ridiculously lush trees of the rainforest.

In exchange for the obnoxious call of the crow, I'm blessed with the melancholy sounds of the black-mandibled toucan.

I gave up my bath and a normal shower for, well, at the moment, I have a house that only has cold water – no hot water in the kitchen or the bathroom. I gave up my bath and normal shower for... a less than normal and less than reliable one.

I still can't find wax paper or sunflower seeds but we do have Lost Coast beer (sometimes!).

I love going to the markets that I frequent the most and the warm greetings I receive from the owners and employees. I also appreciate that I can drop off all my bags behind the cash register so I don't have to drag them around the store as I shop. Small town charm at its best.

I've had manta rays and nursing sharks swim beneath me and laid on the net of my own private catamaran while watching shooting stars light up the night sky as the dark sea water rippled beneath me (okay, not *my* catamaran but I was the only one on it besides the crew... a story for another day).

I traded in a 40" plasma TV for an iPad and a super comfy and huge sofa for a hammock.

We have seasons here...sort of. They don't always happen at the same time of year but trees will lose their leaves and flowers will blossom. My new little house is also surrounded by mango trees...it's going to be one delicious "season"!

The lone howler who lives in the trees is continuing with his attempts to make friends with the troop across the street. Failing each time, but never giving up. His persistence inspires me.

Monkeys play on the roof and run around the terrace; it never gets old. I'm enchanted by these creatures, especially the tiny endangered squirrel monkeys and their delightfully sweet communication squeaks.

Nature is still the ultimate distraction for me, even more so than the hot surfers or the street sweeper. I can spend hours mesmerized, watching the natural world go by.

From sunrise to sunset, life is happening.

I still have everyday dilemmas...

Even today, many years later, people I meet are still so shocked that I live in Costa Rica. They cannot imagine becoming an expatriate and moving so far from everyone they knew. And always, always, always, the question is, *"Did you move there for a guy?"* When I tell them no, they're even more shocked. How could I possibly have moved here all by myself?

3 books in, I know you know that my answer is essentially, "I can do anything I want."

It's nearly impossible to stop me once I've put my mind to something.

Sure, life can insert speed bumps in the process but I was raised to be independent and take care of myself. I don't need a man to help me live or to help me fulfill my life's aspirations, because they're mine to live. *"What century am I living in!"* is a thought I have often.

I have learned to prepare meals within the tiny confines of my kitchen: one square foot of counter space, a hot plate and thankfully a dehydrator that kind friends recently brought me. I have no oven, toaster oven, microwave, dishwasher or even a regular old toaster. I have broken an entire set of salad plates and 2 sets of glasses - a single tiny sink and a dish rack are not my friends.

I realize that small spaces are no big deal for people who live in places like New York, but for this California girl, having my entire house fit into the size of my parent's bedroom suite is still very much a challenge. I'm not looking for a gigantic house. Just something large enough so I don't have to go searching through unpacked plastic bins to find a kitchen utensil because there are no cabinets, closets or drawers... *oh how I miss my junk drawer.*

My washer isn't automatic. It's not manual like a washing board but it falls somewhere in between the two. My refrigerator is also not a "normal" size and because everything must be kept in it, it's always stuffed full.

It's a good day when the utilities are all functioning. But because they continue to go out all the time, meaning no water, no electricity, no internet, I know to keep everything charged and my water pitcher full, chilling in the fridge.

The ATM at the National Bank continues to be unable to deposit checks or cash – only withdrawals allowed. And yet it still seems to take 5 minutes per transaction. The lines at the ATM and inside the bank are never-ending on the 15th and last day of the month. I do not recommend going to the bank on those days unless you're craving a theme park experience, without the fun rollercoaster payoff at the end.

The rain on the tin roof (and lack of insulation much less a ceiling) makes it nearly impossible to hear my clients on the phone so in winter I know to book my client calls in the mornings and hope the storms hold out until the afternoon.

Weird things still happen – like the other day there were no pineapples or cucumbers at my little "wal mart".

I'm still finding some things odd – like how the top ramen is next to the feminine hygiene products or the door locks are installed upside down. When I said things are crazy, backwards and upside down, I mean it literally! Right now, I don't even have door knobs on any of the doors in my house, interior or exterior.

My housekeeper can't seem to understand that the sponge with the handle full of soap is the tool that I want to use for my dishes, *not* the tub of axion soap and a sponge that was left under the sink by the last tenant.

My current computer only holds a 20-minute charge at this point, the video doesn't work, the USB port is a bit wonky and the WiFi switch is super sensitive, so it turns off and on of its own accord.

My residency application is still pending. Nearly

five years of living here and my application continues to gather dust on someone's desk while they enjoy their afternoon coffee.

I still don't have health insurance or property insurance. Every time I leave the house, I hide many of my personal belongings in various places and often times forget where I put something.

While the above might sound like a laundry list of tradeoffs, upgrades, compromises and complaints, acknowledging every part is how I make the grass green, exactly where I am.

I acknowledge the weeds and appreciate the wildflowers, in equal measure. It's all part of my life and wishing it away would be a disservice and create imbalance.

Choices. We each have a choice. Every day. I choose to show up and do my work, to live my purpose in creating more harmony in the world and to support others in doing the same. I choose to live a beautiful life...on *my* terms.

It may not look like your life, and while some of you may be thinking that my life doesn't look all that bad... trust me, you don't want my life.

That being said, I remind myself *and you* that our life is the product of our choices, so if you wish for something different, trust yourself, throw on your brave pants and make the leap.

Don't just go to the edge of your comfort zone but take one more step. And then another.

CHRISSY GRUNINGER

Choose to mindfully swim upstream, go against the current. Be bold, wildhearted and free.

As you've seen from my books, what you'll learn about yourself is invaluable.

I need to add here though...

It isn't always easy; there are still days when I feel alone, unsupported, afraid or unsure of what I'm going to do next. But then I remember to return to the present. To pause, take a breath and know that I am here. Now.

My yoga practice, on and off the mat, carries me through the more challenging days and reminds me to practice patience, compassion, and perseverance.

This moment, this breath, today. That is how I choose to live. Not in the past, not in the future. Today. The present moment.

Am I comfortable? Honestly, not always. But then I say to myself a quote that I've often heard from Buddhism: *May I be like the lotus, choosing to live with ease in the muddy water.*

The beautiful lotus flower blooms even though it's surrounded by mud. That's how I choose to live my life – to blossom, even in, and perhaps especially because of, the discomfort.

Being simply sanguine is my daily mantra.

To remain positive amongst the chaos both

external and within myself. Building up my strength allows me to find peace in the less than comfortable moments.

I still have moments of crisis, when the world seems like it's crumbling around me, but I'm also able to recognize those moments as times for growth, challenging myself to learn and do more than I could have imagined.

It's not easy, but it's necessary. Not only for my sanity but for me to able to continue to show up and do the work in the world that I want to do.

There are also still some things that make me sad, frustrated, angry or just plain confused. For example, when my housekeeper looks at all my many books in awe and tells me that *Ticos don't read* (which explains the lack of libraries and bookstores). I can't imagine not valuing books and not just because I write them!

It's also still a jarring sight to see the many young girls walking around town, during school hours in their uniforms, with toddlers in tow. It's also beyond me to explain to my visiting friends why the locals get up from their spot on the beach and leave all their trash behind or why so many men urinate on the side of the road. It's definitely an example of how my values differ from those around me, which helps me to ground into them, rather than change to be accepted.

It helps me to remember a great line from Chimamanda Ngozi Adichie's TED Talk, *The danger of a single story*. She says, "*When we reject the single story, when we realize that there is never a single story about any place, we regain a kind of paradise."*

There are an abundance of stories to be told, here and everywhere. There is no one way of doing things. There is no one way to live one's life.

With an ever expanding open heart and mind, I understand it's an imperfect world but my choice, my belief, and my *only option* is to THRIVE. To live wildheartedly.

My life's story is complicated and messy, beautiful and unpredictable, with never-ending twists and turns. And it is continuously unfolding before me.

You can have *Pura Vida*, I'll take *mi vida imperfecta* anytime.

In Loving Memory
Harmony
March 1995-March 2013
Thank you for coming with me
on this journey of life.
You are so very missed.

About the Author

Chrissy Gruninger's intention for all that she does is to reflect the harmony, the oneness, in all that exists. Through her writing, she shares what she sees and learns, exploring the many facets of the world around us. She lives a meaningful, wildhearted life; one that is in service to others, providing a voice for those who cannot speak up for themselves.

She is a yoga teacher, happiness mentor and received her Graduate Degree in Integrative Health and Sustainability from Sonoma State

University in 2008. She is a multi-passionate entrepreneur and owns Social [media] Wellness, an online business management firm and ChrissyGruninger.com.

Chrissy empowers individuals in creating more harmony in their lives and supports professionals in creating more harmony in the world. She offers personalized mentoring based on her signature approach, Inherent Harmony, as well as online business management for wellness and eco companies committed to spreading positive energy.

To further explore ways on how to live A Wildhearted Sanguine Life, one that embodies intentional and mindful action, please connect with Chrissy at www.chrissygruninger.com.

Her Living Well Collection and Rich Coast Experiences Collection are available in print or via iBooks and Kindle. These books are designed to teach you to live more intentionally; to experience and become aware of the beauty that is within each of us and all that exists in the world.

Her free 30 day Simply Sanguine Challenge is available at chrissygruninger.com/simply-sanguine-main.

Made in the USA
Las Vegas, NV
27 January 2022